Diary of an Early American Boy:

NOAH BLAKE 1805

Also by ERIC SLOANE

Do and Don't
*A Museum of Early American Tools
The Little Red Schoolhouse
*Age of Barns
ABC Book of Early Americana
Seasons of America Past
Book of Storms
*A Reverence for Wood
Folklore of Early American Weather
A Sound of Bells
Look at the Sky and Know the Weather
Second Barrel
Cracker Barrel
Eric Sloane's Almanac and Weather Forecaster
Eric Sloane's Weather Book
Mister Daniels and the Grange
Return to Taos
American Barns and Covered Bridges
America Yesterday
*Our Vanishing Landscape
*The Spirits of '76
Recollections in Black and White
I Remember America

Published by Ballantine Books

DIARY

of an

EARLY AMERICAN BOY

Noah Blake 1805

ERIC SLOANE

BALLANTINE BOOKS • NEW YORK

Library of Congress Catalog Card Number:
62-18313

ISBN 0-345-24385-4

This edition published by arrangement with
Funk & Wagnalls, Inc.

Manufactured in the United States of America

First Ballantine Books Edition: February 1974
Sixth Printing: January 1979

To my young niece Pam
whose enthusiasm about
the diary gave me the
incentive for doing this book

The DIARY of NOAH BLAKE . . 1805 .

Closed

Open

His ink-pot and Pen.

Author's Note

One time a young boy visited a museum of early American things. There were ladies' bustles and men's wigs and other obsolete things. There were tremendous planes and broadaxes that appeared much too heavy for actual use. There were whole aisles of kitchen equipment and farm tools that no one would care to use now. To the boy, it all looked very much like a neatly arranged and well-cared-for junk yard. He wasn't quite sure what was meant by the title "Americana": all he could think of was, "How dreary life must have been in those days and how unhappy the people must have been, and how glad I am that I live today instead of then."

I am sure that whoever collected and arranged those things did so to excite admiration for the old days; he would have been very displeased with the boy's reaction. Yet I cannot blame the boy, for just as in so many museums of early Americana, the chief attraction of the pieces was made to be *just old age*.

Even now (for I was the little boy), I can feel no reverence for old age. Respect is not due older people for their age and wrinkles or gray hair; respect is due them simply for the things they have learned and for their extra years of experience.

The old-time craftsmen would have been the very first to have junked crude or obsolete things, so why should we seek them and collect them for display as examples of early American life? Indeed, there are ugly things in all ages which should be discarded and forgotten. Only the good things of either the past or the present are worthy of collection.

The good things of the past were not so often *articles* as they were the *manner in which people lived* or the *things that the people thought*. This, of course, is still true; the fine TV sets and modern kitchen equipment we prize now will be junk within a matter of years; the lasting examples of our time will turn out to be the *ways that we live* or the *things that we think.*

For a long while I have collected early American wooden tools— those things that pioneer people fashioned at home. It seems that they put so much of themselves into these implements that just being with them is like being with the people who created them. Closing your hand around a worn wooden hammer handle is very much like reaching back into the years and feeling the very hand that wore it smooth.

And so it is my special pleasure to behold the lines of hand-made things and to see the patina of seasoned wood and to feel a patriotic pride in the good workmanship there.

My collection is not a collection of implements as much as it is a collection of works of art. Many of the pieces would actually win merit in any gallery of sculpture, for when a man creates something he has become a designer, often an artist.

When I show my collection to young people, I am very careful to avoid saying, "See how old these things are." Instead I say, "See how carefully and beautifully people created things in those days. How aware these people were of the kinds of materials they worked with. How aware they were of the time in which they lived; everything is dated and signed. How richly awake they must have been to every moment of each day!"

This book is based upon a diary written in 1805. It was a small wood-backed, leather-bound volume that I found in an ancient house; with it I found a hand-made stone inkwell initialed N.B. I have taken a writer's liberty to imagine a great deal, but I have tried thereby to recreate seasons of activities as they might have been during 1805.

Before reading this book I ask you first to study the sketches on the following pages where I have tried to create the scene of Noah Blake's countryside both before and after he was born. Do compare these two sketches, so that you may better follow the activities at the Blake Homestead during the year of the diary.

If you get the slightest portion of the immense pleasure I got while researching this material, my book will have been worth the while.

Eric Sloane

Weather Hill
Cornwall Bridge
Connecticut

Farm·forged axe.

... *"would win top honor in any Gallery of Sculpture."*

CLAY and STICK CHIMNEY

TEMPORARY BARK ROOF

SOLID SHUTTER

BORNING ROOM

WATERING PLACE

The BLAKE place, 1790

This was the year when Noah was born... the year after Izaak Blake and his wife Rachel built their cabin near Red Man Brook. The bark roofs, the clay-and-stick chimney and the temporary lean-to barn were all replaced. Look at the next picture and see what changes occurred ➔

The **BLAKE** place some time, after 1805 ...

With the help of Noah, Izaac Blake had created a workable homestead. The Indian Trail became a roadway ·· the brook became a source of power to grind corn that grew where once a forest stood ... the shelter became home to an early American boy.

Here, in the condition in which they were found, are Noah Blake's diary, inkwell, and almanac. . . .

The log at the wood pile, the axe supported by it;
The sylvan hut, the vine over the doorway, the space
    cleared for a garden,
The irregular tapping of rain down on the leaves,
    after the storm is lulled,
. . . The sentiment of the huge timbers of old fashion'd
    houses and barns.

WALT WHITMAN

Diary of an Early American Boy:

NOAH BLAKE 1805

Chapter 1

That March dawn in the year 1805 seemed like any other dawn. Yet to Noah there was something different. Clearer and more crimson than a sunset, the morning sun blazed out of the east and struck the four small panes of his window as if they were its prime target. Glass was hard enough to come by in pioneer days, but these panes had special meaning. Made in faraway London, they had been Noah's tenth birthday gift from his mother and father five years ago. Before Noah's tenth birthday the window had been covered with one pine slab that swung outward on leather hinges along the top. This made it possible to leave the window open all during warm weather except for the stormiest days; the rain fell away from the opening, running off the pine slab as if it were an awning. In the winter the slab was closed upon a room that would have been totally dark except for the light of a candle.

The four glass panes of Noah's window were unlike present-day glass.

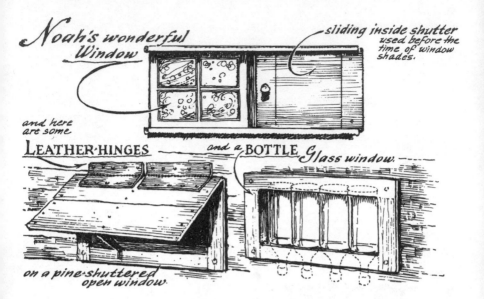

Noah's wonderful Window

sliding inside shutter used before the time of window shades.

and here are some

LEATHER·HINGES — *and a* BOTTLE *Glass window.*

on a pine-shuttered open window.

Being hand-made, they were full of irregular ripples and bubbles that changed the appearance of everything viewed through them. The moon was a special treat, assuming almost every shape but its own whenever you moved the slightest bit. In even a slight breeze the straightest trees wiggled and swayed as if they were blowing in a big storm.

There was only one other glass window in the house, and that window had six panes in it. Those six panes and Noah's four made up the set of ten pieces of glass which was once the allowable limit in a house, without a tax charge. Some people saved the glass tax by using oiled paper for their windowpanes, but that didn't let much light through; others made their windows of rows of bottles cemented into the windowframes, though all too little light filtered through the greenish glass of the old bottles. The double thickness of rounded bottle glass, however, was good protection against arrows and even gunshot. Of course you couldn't open a bottle-glass window.

Glass-paned windows were actually so rare in the early country houses that people often carried their windows with them from house to house whenever they moved. You often rented a house "without benefit of glass!" Few of us today could imagine how a simple glass window could bring such unending joy to a child.

Curtains were almost unknown in the back country houses, but every window had its shutter. Some shutters closed at night from the outside, but Noah's shutter simply slid back and forth from the inside, a solid wooden slab.

Noah's view of his window each morning was usually from his special "doorway" in the folds of his big patchwork quilt. Father and Mother wore nightcaps like everyone else of that time, but since early childhood Noah had enjoyed making a "blanket tent" over his head and, like the cow in the barn, making his own breath and body heat keep the tent warm.

At the foot of the bed where tomorrow's clothing was folded and packed beside a stone bed-warmer during winter, there was still a glow of warmth from last night's heat. But the piece of hot soapstone wrapped in a towel had about done its work for the night, and the coldness of forest dawn had begun to penetrate. The hearth of the fireplace in the big room (that space reserved by Noah's parents for morning dressing) was losing its heat fast.

Except during winter weather, this was the moment when Noah usually grabbed his clothing from its place beneath the covers, tucked it all under his nightshirt, and bounded across the road into the barn "before the coldness could catch up with him." Into the barn he would go and make Bessie the cow or Daniel the ox rise up and move away from their soft beds of hay. Then, standing in the warmed flat spot, he would go about the business of dressing for the day.

But today was a special sort of day. It was the twenty-fifth of March, not only Noah's birthday, but also the first day of the early American farming-man's Spring. The almanac calendar simply read, "Monday, the twenty-fifth," but to many farmers who kept the old European customs, it was New Year Day; so farm accounts and farm diaries were often started at that time. This day was to be marked by Noah's first entry in his new diary.

The sunlight came through the windowpanes and fell upon the diary; it was bound in calf and wrapped once around with a leather thong just like father's ledger book. Its pages were crisp and freshly made at the new paper mill in town. Alongside it was a little stone well of butternut ink that Noah had made himself and put there last night, ready for this special morning. Reaching out from his warm tent of blankets, Noah dipped a crow quill into the ink and held it poised for a moment, thinking. Then he wrote in a clear hand at the top of the first page:

NOAH BLAKE, *my book*

March the twenty-fifth, Year of Our Lord 1805
Given to me by my Father Izaak Blake and my Mother
Rachel upon the fifteenth year of my Life.

In keeping with the custom for drying ink, he sprinkled the wet writing with sand. After admiring the freshly sanded page with its first written message, Noah blew away the sand and closed the book. The first day's entry would go on the next page and that would be added at bedtime by candlelight. Feeling beneath the covers for his clothing, he exploded out of his warm "tent" and headed for his springtime dressing room in the barn.

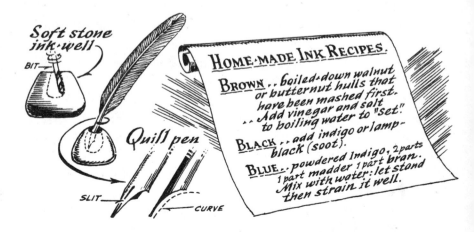

Soft stone ink·well
BIT
Quill pen
SLIT
CURVE

HOME·MADE INK RECIPES.
BROWN .. boiled·down walnut or butternut hulls that have been mashed first. .. Add vinegar and salt to boiling water to "set."
BLACK .. add indigo or lamp-black (soot).
BLUE .. powdered Indigo, 2 parts 1 part madder 1 part bran.. Mix with water: let stand then strain it well.

Chapter 2

25 : *A cold and windy day. Neighbor Adams with son Robert stopp'd by. We drank mead * and mint tea. No work done this day. Father is going to the woodlot behind the barn tomorrow for floor timbers. I shall assist him.*

26 : *A light snow fell which Father believes will be the last of the winter. We fell'd a fine oak and rolled it upon rails for Spring seasoning. Mother is joyous at the thought of a good wood floor.*

One might wonder why a floor should be planned for a house already existing. Like the earliest country houses, which were built hurriedly, the Blake house still had a plain dirt floor. The earth was pounded hard and swept smooth each day. Housewives sometimes made designs on their dirt floors to amuse their families; Rachel Blake often did this.

---

* *Recipes for the three types of mead may be found on page 144 of* THE SEASONS OF AMERICA PAST *by Eric Sloane.*

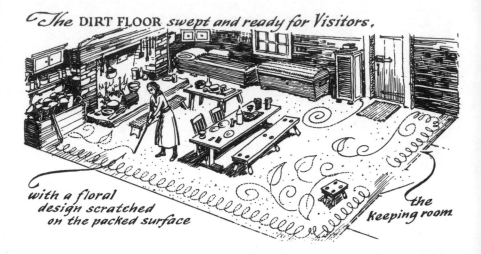

The DIRT FLOOR *swept and ready for Visitors,* with a floral design scratched on the packed surface

the Keeping room

"Get the floor ready for visitors," Izaak would say, and the procedure which followed would amuse anyone of today. Rachel would sweep the hard-packed floor and then with a stick she would scratch designs upon it in the manner of a decorative carpet. The Blake's "dirt carpet" changed in design according to the occasion: at Christmas there was a holly design and on a birthday there might be a birthday greeting scratched on the floor near the hearth. The whole idea was unending fun, yet even Noah looked forward to the more civilized pleasure of a hard, dry oak-plank flooring instead of earth.

> 27 : *Father was wrong about the weather, for it snowed again today. We kept within the house, sharping and making ready tools for the year's farming.*

Just as boys are taught the proper handling of firearms today, the early American child soon learned how to handle an axe and keep it ready for use. It was as important to know how not to handle an axe, and the first lesson was to lay your blade to the wall or sink it well into a soft log for safety's sake.

The axe was the pioneer's most important tool; a man could walk into the forest with nothing but his axe, yet fashion snares to catch game, fell trees, and fit them into a cabin. He could even clear brush for growing a garden and by holding an axe blade in his palm, he could use the sharp blade in the manner of a knife and whittle with it.

In very cold weather Izaak would heat his blade before using it to make it less brittle; when he was through using it for the day he rubbed it carefully with fat. Axe handles often cracked or broke, but there was always a new one charring and seasoning close to the hearth.

Noah's axe had no flat head or "poll" like the axe of today. The axe handle was long and straight; the curved handle that we know so well now didn't appear for another fifty years.

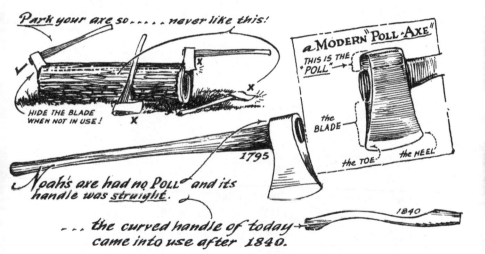

Park your axe so..... never like this!

a MODERN "POLL·AXE"

THIS IS THE "POLL"→

HIDE THE BLADE WHEN NOT IN USE!

the BLADE

the TOE·   the HEEL

1795

Noah's axe had no POLL and its handle was straight.

the TOE·   the HEEL

1840

...the curved handle of today→ came into use after 1840.

28 : Snow stopp'd during the night but it is very cold. My window glass is frosty and my ink froze.
29 : I moved bed into the Loft for warmth. It is good to be with Mother and Father but I do miss my good window.

30 : *Worked in the forge barn. The Loft proved too warm so I moved back into my room.*

31 : *A fine Sunday. The roads were bad and we could not get to Meeting. Had Service to our Lord at home.*

Before Noah moved into the wing which was once his borning room, he had slept on a loft at one end of the big keeping-room. Sleeping lofts were made by placing planks on the cross beams of a cabin to form a sort of balcony overhead. A ladder gave access to the loft, and in the early days when a pioneer would leave the door of his windowless cabin open for ventilation, he would pull the ladder up after him for protection against Indians and wild animals.

Sleeping-loft ladders were always a challenge to wood craftsmen because there are so many ways to make a ladder. Some ladders folded into one fat round pole; others were heavy and permanent—the forerunners of built-in staircases. Some were just pegs driven into the wall.

A few years after a cabin had been built, when there was more time

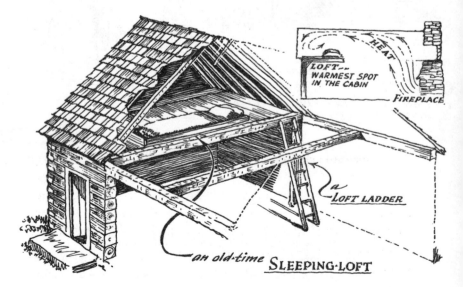

LOFT—WARMEST SPOT IN THE CABIN

HEAT

FIREPLACE

a LOFT LADDER

an old-time SLEEPING-LOFT

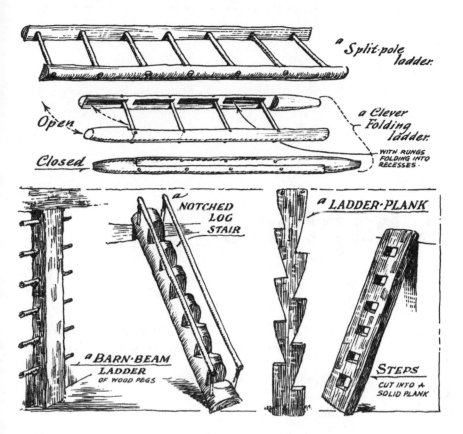

a Split-pole ladder.

a Clever Folding ladder.

Open

Closed

WITH RUNGS
FOLDING INTO
RECESSES.

a NOTCHED LOG STAIR

a LADDER-PLANK

a BARN-BEAM LADDER OF WOOD PEGS

STEPS
CUT INTO A
SOLID PLANK

for remodeling and refining it, the crossbeams were often covered and made into a flat ceiling. Then the place where the sleeping loft had been became part of an attic room, and the old-time loft bed became a thing of the past. But country boys still found great pleasure in ladders and lofts and the game of pulling the ladder up to protect themselves against imaginary bears or Indians who might come in the open door of the room below.

11

Chapter 3

*1 : Robert Adams came by in his Father's sleigh to take me
to the Adams place. I shall help them for the week with
maple sugaring.*

2 : Worked at the Adams place.

3 : do. (ditto)

4 : do.

5 : do.

6 : do.

*7 : Palm Sunday. Went to Meeting with the Adams and re-
turned home with Mother and Father. I earned a tub of
sweetening for my week's work. It is good to be home
again.*

Noah's "tub of sweetening" was a wooden sugar-bucket of thick
maple syrup which was his pay for the help he had given to the Adams
family. No pay could be more appreciated, for sweets and sweetening
were rare things in the pantry closet of 1805. At that time there was no
such thing in all America as candy as we know it now, for the word was

MAPLE·SAP *Bucket*

SPILE *or spout of sumac hollowed out with a hot wire.*

and The soft sugar
TUB
which was part of Noah's pay.

Plug for drawing off "Sugar molasses."

either a verb meaning "to sweeten" or it referred to broken pieces of sugar.

"We have *candy* for dessert today," Rachel Blake would say, and she would place on the dinner table a bowl of hard loaf sugar, with either a "sugar-hammer" or a pair of "sugar scissors" to cut it with.

"The wooden tub was part of my salary," Noah said. "So I'll not have to return it. I'd like to give that to you, Mother."

"And who," asked Rachel Blake, "Did you meet at the sugaring?"

"There were a great many people," replied Noah. "Some I've never seen before. Mrs. Adams tended the stirring and boiling along with a new girl named Sarah Trowbridge. The boys and men collected buckets and sledded the sap back to the sugar house."

Rachel noted a peculiar interest in Noah's voice. "A new girl, did you say?"

"Yes," Noah answered with some attempt to bring attention back to the sugar-bucket, "just a new girl from the south to help Mrs. Adams with the sugaring and farm chores."

> 8 : *The snow has gone and seasonable weather for Spring business has arrived. I finished the winter's lot of nail-making and put the forge to rights.*

In the little forge barn half-way down to the bridge (see the 1790 diagram below), Izaak had earned most of the money needed around the homestead. Not that any early American had great need for cash, as most things were traded; but a good farmer always had a cash crop or some paying trade other than farming. Izaak was a nail-maker. He had taught Noah the art of making hand-wrought nails by letting him pump the bellows of the forge as a little fellow; now and then he actually hammered or broke the iron nail rods.

"Some day," said Izaak, "we will have a water mill right about here, and there will be a big mill-wheel to take your place pumping the bellows. By then you'll be an expert yourself." As a matter of fact, Noah was already an expert.

By the time he reached his fifteenth birthday he could make upward of nine hundred nails a day, and he seldom went over the professional four strokes of the hammer to flatten out the heads.

"As soon as we have the new bridge done so we can haul it over," Izaak told Noah, "we shall get the new water wheel and begin building the

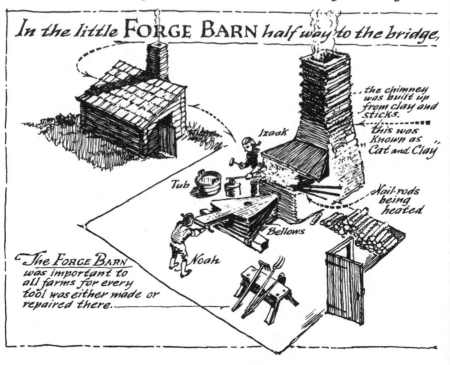

In the little FORGE BARN *half way to the bridge,*

.. the chimney was built up from clay and sticks.

this was known as Cat and Clay

Izaak

Nail-rods being heated

Tub

Bellows

Noah

The FORGE BARN was important to all farms for every tool was either made or repaired there.

mill." Mr. Beach, the carpenter and joiner, had been working on the Blake mill-wheel for almost a year and had promised to have it done by this spring.

Actually, the new bridge and a new mill would be twin projects, because as soon as the mill was ready people would want to come by wagon to buy ironware and nails, and there would have to be a bridge strong enough for the heaviest wagons. Many an American town grew up in just this way, around a lone mill that had its own bridge. That is why you will find so many towns named after some mill, such as the many Miltons (Mill Town), Millvilles, Milbrooks, and so on.

The reader might be interested in knowing just how wrought-iron nails were made and what Noah had to learn about the trade. So this two-page spread of drawings will give you a "nut-shell" lesson in early American nail-making.

9 : Flooding all but washed our bridge away. Father says the new bridge beams are seasoned and ready. When the wa-

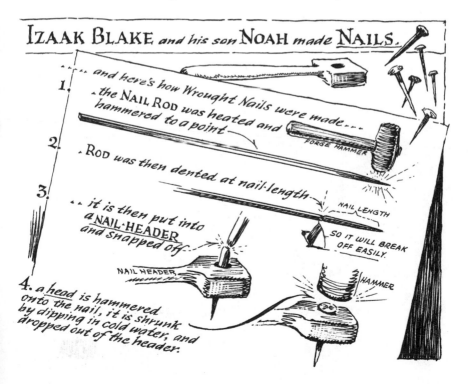

IZAAK BLAKE *and his son* NOAH *made* NAILS.

1. *... and here's how Wrought Nails were made ... the* NAIL ROD *was heated and hammered to a point*

FORGE HAMMER

2. *. ROD was then dented at nail-length*

NAIL LENGTH

SO IT WILL BREAK OFF EASILY.

3. *... it is then put into a* NAIL·HEADER *and snapped off.*

NAIL HEADER

HAMMER

4. *a head is hammered onto the nail, it is shrunk by dipping in cold water, and dropped out of the header.*

ters subside, he shall begin to erect it. We are shaping up the abutments.

10 : *Worked on the bridge abutments. Daniel helped with the bigger stones.*

11 : *do.*

12 : *Good Friday. It rained all day. Brook went up.*

13 : *Bluebirds arrived. We finished the abutments without help of Mr. Adams and his son Robert who came by to assist. River lower.*

14 : *Easter Sunday. A fine Service. Saw Sarah Trowbridge the new girl at the Adams. She is very pretty.*

The little bridge across Red Man Brook was nothing more than two very long tree trunks with planks set atop to walk across. It had lasted ten years, but in the meantime Izaak had prepared a set of truss beams ready for erection as a new bridge as soon as Noah was old enough and strong enough to help.

"The bridge will be a big memory in the boy's life," Izaak had said, "and he will want to have taken part in putting it up."

Like most masonry of early American times, the bridge abutments were built in "dry wall" fashion, which merely meant that no cement

IZAAK BLAKE *and his son build the Abutments.*

where the New Bridge will go.

DANIEL THE OX

A STONE BEING MOVED

Sliding a stone

WITH A FULCRUM (1.) AND LEVER (2.)

RED MAN BROOK

OLD TRAIL

Planks to slide stones on.

Things were sledded *during summer* *by* STONE·BOAT

was used. The old-timers had a knack of fitting stones together so cleverly that no binding at all was necessary. This art of "dry-masonry" used to be so well known that you could just look at a wall or a foundation and recognize it as the work of a particular builder.

All the stones for the Blake bridge were fitted together by Izaak, but the actual moving of the heaviest stones was accomplished with a lever-pole fulcrum (see the drawing) which was operated by Daniel the ox. You might wonder how the pioneers moved some of the great stones that you see in old walls and foundations; the secret was simply in their ability to *slide* things. A two-ton slab of rock that could not be lifted or carted by wagon, could be slid to location with ease just by waiting for winter and *sliding* the stone over ice. Almost no heavy farm loads were hauled on wheels; that was put off till winter when the loads could be slid across the countryside on sled runners. For each wagon the old-time farmer had, he had about four sleds. Even smaller stones were thrown on a flat wooden slab known as a "stone-boat" and slid across the grass during summer, with much less effort than it would take to lift them onto a wagon and cart them on wheels.

Mr. Adams and his son came by to help with the final stone work, but found that they were more in the way than anything else.

"The way Noah handles that lever for you," said Adams, "I guess you'll not be needing us. But when it's time to raise the bridge timbers, we'll be on hand."

> *15 : Father used Daniel this morning to set the bridge beams in place for homing the joints. I tried my hand at spring plowing in the afternoon, with Daniel.*

17

16 : *More plowing. Father still setting up the trusses. He says the joints have swollen with the rains and need new chisel-ling.*

17 : *do. Weather fine.*

18 : *do.*

19 : *Finished plowing. Father has the bridge trusses ready for raising. Tomorrow I shall go to the Adams and ask them to come upon Saturday the next.*

20 : *Spent the day at the Adams. They shall certainly assist with the bridge next Saturday. Sarah Trowbridge did the cooking and she is most excellent.*

21 : *First Sunday past Easter. The Meeting House was very cold. I visited with Sarah after the Service.*

"Setting the timbers in place" and "driving the joints home" were well-known procedures in the days when men built their own barns. The complete skeleton of any building was laid out upon the ground and fastened together loosely with wooden nails (called tree-nails or "trunnels") before raising the sections up and fastening them together.

The drawing shows how Izaak Blake had put together two complete kingpost trusses, ready to be erected into the final bridge. The beams were pounded into place on the ground with a very heavy hammer called a "commander" or "beetle," and then the wooden pins were inserted and hammered into place. Nowadays we assume that people once used wooden pins because it was too hard to make nails or spikes. But metal nails would have either rusted away or split the wood, so wood against wood made a much better fastening. It breathed with weather changes and finally welded itself together into the best possible union. Even today you may find oak trunnels fastening together two barn beams that are solid and firm after two centuries, while a spike would have rusted away long ago and rotted the wood next to it.

It seemed that Noah had taken a great liking to Sarah Trowbridge; although he had had little time for visiting, the two-hour-long church service afforded him plenty of time for admiring her and seeing her in her best dress. You might wonder why his diary mentions that "the

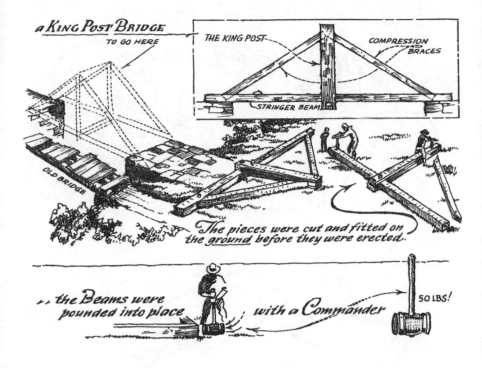

a KING POST BRIDGE
TO GO HERE

THE KING POST

COMPRESSION BRACES

STRINGER BEAM

OLD BRIDGE

The pieces were cut and fitted on the ground before they were erected.

.. the Beams were pounded into place   with a Commander   50 LBS!

Meeting House was very cold," until we remember that even in the early 1800's it was still considered improper to put a stove in a place of worship. People came to church in great fur coats and lap robes; the preacher himself often stood on a tin of hot coals and wore heavy fur mittens while he conducted services.

The long drive to church during winter was made comfortable by a small charcoal stove under the lap robes, and when you entered church you carried your stove with you!

> 22 : Day spent in forge barn fashioning trunnels for bridge. Did forty.
> 23 : Rain and wind. Worked in the garden sowing pease (peas) and beans.

19

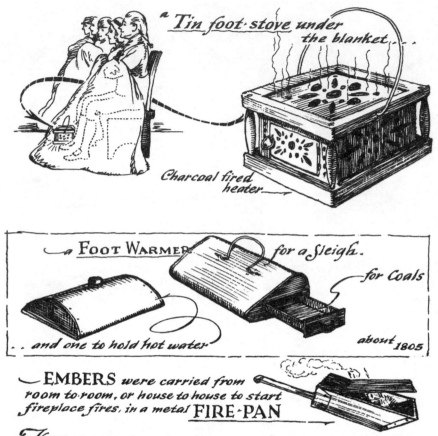

"*Tin foot-stove under the blanket*...

Charcoal fired heater.

a FOOT WARMER *for a Sleigh.*

for Coals

... and one to hold hot water

about 1805

EMBERS *were carried from room to room, or house to house to start fireplace fires, in a metal* FIRE-PAN

The FIRE-PAN *also serviced charcoal foot-warmers in churches.*

24 : Rain stopped and brook is down. Prepared the beams and we put them in place for Saturday's work.

25 : Mr. Thoms came by with a new rope from his walk. I have seldom seen so long and white a rope.

26 : Rain again. Too wet to work in the garden but we thinn'd brush, and we pruned in the woodlot with hooks.

27 : The Adams arrived with six townspeople at sunrise. We

set the stringers and put the kingposts in place. We have made a fine bridge. Father put a brush atop the posts and we all sang and drank. Sarah brought a cake. One man fell into the brook but he was not hurt. We knocked down the old bridge, which made me feel a little sad.

28 : Without yet a floor in the new bridge, we could not yet proceed over it to Sunday Meeting so held Service at home.

Mr. Thoms's "walk" was the place where he made his rope. Rope-walks were sometimes a quarter of a mile long; they were usually at the edge of town where traffic would not interfere with the business of rope-winding. In the early days, for example, New York's main street, Broadway, ended as a rope-walk which extended uptown for about two thousand feet and into a meadow.

The rope-spinner had a large bundle of fiber gathered loosely around his waist; he pulled out strands from this and wove them into cords, walking backward along the rope-walk as he worked. Another man wound the twisted cords into rope.

It was once the custom for rope-makers to rent rope for special purposes, so we might presume that Mr. Thoms rented Izaak the rope for raising his bridge. A backwoods farmer seldom had any use for such great lengths of rope. Moreover, the expense made good rope a rare thing around the farmyard.

On the twenty-sixth day of April, Noah's diary said that they pruned trees "with hooks," and that statement harks back to an ancient phrase which most of us still use, to get anything "*by hook or by crook.*" As dead tree limbs harbor insects and disease, the old-timers were careful to remove as much deadwood from a stand of trees as they could, and people used to walk through the forest with a hooked stick much like a shepherd's staff; the hook was used to pull dead branches from trees.

Very early house leases forbade the tenant to cut trees for firewood, although he was always allowed "as much wood as could be taken by *hook* or *crook.*" How long this legal phrase has lived, although few of us realize whence it came!

Another ancient custom is seen in Izaak's "putting a brush on top" of the new structure. Even nowadays you will see workmen put a small tree or bush on the top of a new roof when it has been completed. That ceremony always calls for a round of drinks for the builders, and although we don't seem to know why we do it, we say it is "just to give

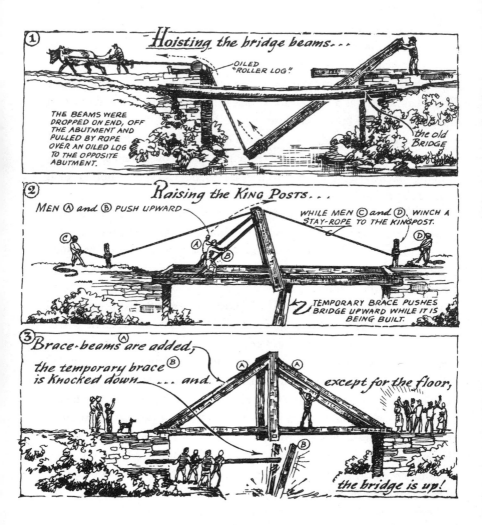

① *Hoisting the bridge beams...*

OILED "ROLLER LOG"!

THE BEAMS WERE DROPPED ON END, OFF THE ABUTMENT AND PULLED BY ROPE OVER AN OILED LOG TO THE OPPOSITE ABUTMENT.

the old BRIDGE

② *Raising the King Posts...*

MEN Ⓐ and Ⓑ PUSH UPWARD

WHILE MEN Ⓒ and Ⓓ, WINCH A STAY-ROPE TO THE KINGPOST.

TEMPORARY BRACE PUSHES BRIDGE UPWARD WHILE IT IS BEING BUILT.

③ *Brace-beams are added;*

the temporary brace Ⓑ is knocked down .... and.

except for the floor,

the bridge is up!

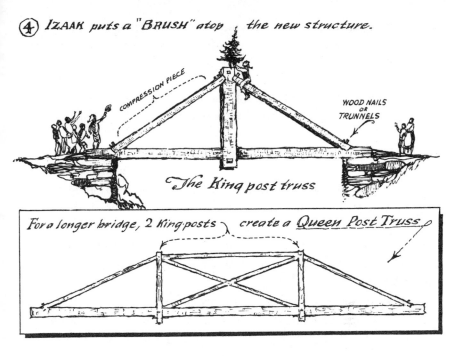

④ IZAAK *puts a* "BRUSH" *atop the new structure.*

COMPRESSION PIECE

WOOD NAILS
OR
TRUNNELS

The King post truss

For a longer bridge, 2 King posts create a Queen Post Truss

the house luck." That tree tacked atop a new building goes all the way back to Druid lore when men worshipped trees!

Whether the "raising" was of a home or a church or a bridge, people used to come from all around to help. The women brought food and drink while the men just brought their strong backs. Children used to make up rhymes to recite or songs to sing at the raisings, and a house often got its name through one of these impromptu house-raising songs.

Often the house-raising song was sewed into a sampler by some enterprising young girl and presented to the owner at the house-warming when the owners moved in. For example, there is on record a house in Rochester, New Hampshire which was so celebrated in verse:

> "*Flower of the Plain* is the name of this frame,
> We've had exceeding good luck in raising the Same."

Sarah brought with her a rhyme for the occasion, and though she had not sewed it into a sampler, she had made several copies of it and everyone sang:

> "On Red Man Brook we've raised a frame
> And *Noah Blake Bridge* will be its name."

If you look at the drawing of the bridge-raising, you can see how the timbers were put in place and raised into a permanent truss, first with the help of Daniel the ox, and then with the help of the Adams family and other neighbors. You may also see how the slanted beams tend to push against each other as "compression pieces" and lift the kingpost. The kingpost truss was the simplest of bridge trusses, followed by the "queenpost truss" which was simply two kingposts put together for a longer span.

Just about the time that Noah and his father built their bridge, many Americans were designing different kinds of trusses, getting their designs patented, and selling their plans at a dollar a foot to bridge builders. Some of America's first fortunes were earned by these enterprising designers.

29 : A sloppy day. Started splitting boards for bridge floor.
30 : Still working on the bridge floor. Father splits while I saw.

the SPLIT·AXE *for splitting logs* (ALSO CALLED HOLZAXT)
wedgelike head for hitting
1800

Chapter 4

1 : The First of May! We have nearly finished the bridge floor but we must abandon this work for the garden. Father is planting corn.

2 : A sour chilly day. Stayed indoors.

3 : We finished the bridge floor in time for the Adams to be first across it. They brought with them a paper with news about the Great Permanent Bridge in Philadelphia. Sarah did not come with them. Yesterday was the Birth Day of new pigs at the Adams.

4 : A splendid day. Went to the Adams to see the pigs. Sarah looked very well.

We certainly might wonder if Noah went to the Adamses to see the new pigs or to see Sarah. He didn't remark about the pigs, but Sarah seemed to "look very well!"

One of the satisfactions of working with wood is the ability to split it expertly. If you season (dry) wood properly and place a wedge in the right place, you can split shingles or rails or boards from it with a single good blow; such a cut might take hours if tried with a saw!

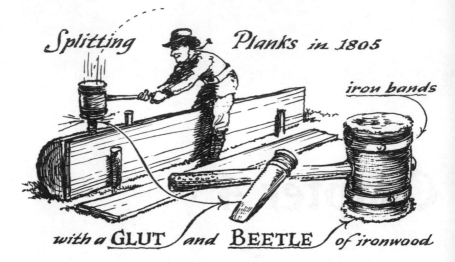

Splitting **Planks** *in 1805*

iron bands

with a <u>GLUT</u> *and* <u>BEETLE</u> *of ironwood*

"Here," said Izaak, "is a saw for cutting across the ends of the boards. You do that while I split the logs into planks."

Axes were too valuable ever to be used as hammers—even now a good woodsman will never hammer a wedge with the head of an axe when there is a sledge hammer to do the job. Izaak's hammer was made of hardwood. Even his wedges were made of hardwood; they were known as "gluts."

"Do we nail the boards down soon?" asked Noah.

"No," said his father. "The trick is just to lay them down loosely so they won't warp. Then you place a roadway going the opposite way across the top. Nails would only split boards and rust the cracks into rot. Loose boards weather best."

"I know," said Noah, "that a good carpenter doesn't use nails unless he has to. I just forgot."

"If we can do it," said Izaak, with some pride in his voice, "we will finish this bridge without the use of iron at all. Not even one nail will be used!"

Just as the last floor board was laid down, a shout sounded from on top of the trail and Mr. Adams came into view, his son Robert close behind him.

"It is beautiful," they called out. "May we be the first visitors across?"

"Welcome!" said Izaak. "This will call for a celebration! We shall let you cross even before the cross boards are done with, and then we shall all go to the house for hot tea."

Rachel had seen them coming, and tea was ready by the time they arrived. At the house, Mr. Adams brought out a copy of the latest Philadelphia newspaper which he said would be of the greatest interest to Izaak. The newspaper was a single folded sheet (all newspapers and even letters were single sheets of paper, because you paid full postage for each sheet no matter how small or large) and the name of the paper was *The Pennsylvania Packet and General Advertiser.*

"Look here," said Mr. Adams, "and you may read the latest news about the new Permanent Bridge over the Schuylkill. They are going to cover it over like a house! They say that any bridge with a cover on it will last twice as long as one without a cover. Mark my words, every wooden bridge in America will be adding a roof and sides before long! What about covering yours?"

Izaak read through the account silently and seriously; during the quiet, everyone pondered the new idea and they had a mind's eye picture of how the new bridge would look "with a house around it."

"I think it's a good idea," said Izaak. "We can put the roof on it first, then we can add siding before the winter comes. I guess if those Philadelphia builders can have a covered bridge, we can have one, too."

"Wow!" howled Noah. "What an idea! We can get out of the rain in it. Maybe we can even have windows in it."

"I suppose you'll want curtains too," added Rachel with a chuckle.

Today, covered bridges are treated as a curiosity so antique that many of us believe that they began during the Revolutionary War or even before that. Yet until the Schuylkill Bridge added its covering, there

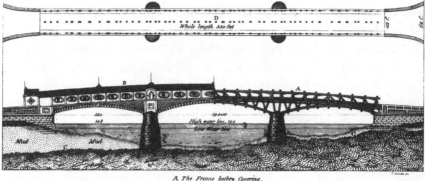

Architectural Plan and Elevation of the Schuylkill P. Bridge.

A *The Frame before Covering.*
B *The Cover.*
C *Surface of the Rock at the Bottom.*
D *Platform.*

were no covered bridges at all in America. The idea took over so quickly, however, it seemed that almost overnight all of our wooden bridges became covered and the famous "early American covered bridge" was born. The stories we may hear of how "George Washington crossed over this or that covered bridge," are of course, untrue.

The Blake covered bridge could have been the second one in America, as the Schuylkill Bridge put on its roof during the year 1805. By that time Washington had died; so an American covered bridge was never even viewed by our first president. But, as this book is being written, there are still over fifteen hundred of these bridges left.

> 5 : *First Sunday to pass across new bridge to Meeting.*
> 6 : *Father and I layed the cross-planks upon the bridge. He says it will take a month before they become dry and lay right. It will be my chore to turn them over when they warp or bend.*
> 7 : *Some of my pease are up! But spring is backward.*

28

8 : Helped Father with stump-pulling to enlarge the corn-
field. Started plowing this evening.
9 : Plowed all the day. High winds from the west.
10 : Took the day off and went into the woods looking for
hoop wood. Found muskrat den. Will set snares soon.

Both stump-pulling and finding "hoop wood" were spring chores of early times. After the ground had heaved and settled when winter was done, roots were looser and the big tree stumps were then easier to pull out. The tough roots were almost impossible to burn, so farmers used to push them into a fence formation that wasn't very pretty to look at, but lasted for many more years than an ordinary fence. Even now in Canada and on some remote farms, you will find good root-fences almost a century old!

Noah helped his father with the stumps for a while, but with the help of Daniel the ox, Izaak found he could do the job alone, so Noah disappeared into the woods for an afternoon jaunt. He came back laden with an armful of newly cut poles.

"What," exclaimed Izaak, "are you going to do with all of those?"

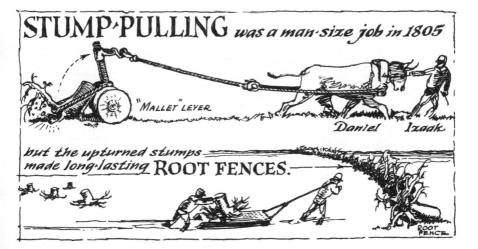

STUMP·PULLING *was a man-size job in 1805*

"MALLET" LEVER

Daniel   Izaak

but the upturned stumps
made long-lasting ROOT FENCES.

ROOT FENCE

"I guess you haven't heard about the new cooper in the village," replied Noah. "He told Robert and me that he could use all the good hoop wood that we can supply him with. Robert and I shall keep a

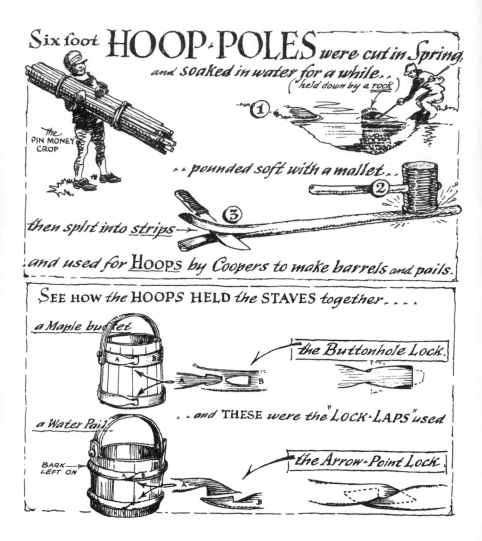

Six foot HOOP-POLES were cut in Spring, and soaked in water for a while..
(held down by a rock)
①

THE PIN MONEY CROP

..pounded soft with a mallet..
②

then split into strips →
③

and used for HOOPS by Coopers to make barrels and pails.

SEE HOW the HOOPS HELD the STAVES together....

a Maple bucket
the Buttonhole Lock.

..and THESE were the "LOCK-LAPS" used

a Water Pail
BARK LEFT ON
the Arrow-Point Lock

supply soaking in a bank over in Indian Brook meadow. Then whenever we go to the village and need a bit of spending money, we shall pick up a bundle of hoop wood and sell it to Mr. Minor. He's the new cooper."

In May, when black ash and hickory are alive with new sap, six-foot poles were cut from the saplings in the swamplands. After a good soaking, the poles were pounded soft and "rived" or cut into strips for making barrel hoops. You just pounded the softened wood strip around a barrel and when it dried, you had a hoop that was as hard as iron and even outlasted metal.

> *11 : Rain. Split shingle wood for a roof on the new bridge.*
> *12 : Sunday. Sarah walked home from Meeting with me to admire the new bridge. I walked back with her.*
> *13 : A sour day. Worked indoors again splitting wood.*
> *14 : Rain again. Brook ran high but the new bridge is much higher than flood level.*
> *15 : Saw flock of bluebirds. There are blossoms on the pea vine in the garden. Warm day.*
> *16 : do.*

During the spring rains, farmers found time for doing indoor chores such as repairing equipment or splitting firewood under cover. Noah seems to have found lots of time for splitting shingles and firewood during this rainy spring week.

Few of us today would think of wood splitting as anything but a tedious chore, but when one learns to do it well, there is a certain joy involved. Striking your axe in an exact spot, watching a log divide miraculously into segments and squares with single blows, or even learning to stack a simple pile of wood correctly, gives pleasure to the art of woodsmanship.

Noah's diary doesn't mention what tool he used to split shingles with, but we know it must have been a "frow." This was a heavy knife blade attached to a handle and struck on the top with a "maul" or heavy club. If you take any two- or three-foot pine or cedar log and let it dry for a year, it needs only a frow to divide it nicely into a dozen or so fine shingles.

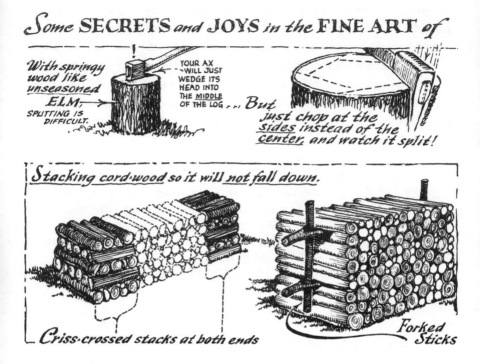

Some SECRETS and JOYS in the FINE ART of

With springy wood like unseasoned ELM, SPLITTING IS DIFFICULT.

YOUR AX WILL JUST WEDGE ITS HEAD INTO THE MIDDLE OF THE LOG ... *But just chop at the sides instead of the center, and watch it split!*

Stacking cord·wood so it will *not fall down*.

Criss·crossed stacks at both ends

Forked Sticks

If you will notice in the large drawing of the Blake Place in 1790, the house had a bark roof. Bark roofs were easier to make in a hurry, and as shingle material had to be dried for a year or more before splitting, we might assume that proper wood shingles were added to the Blake place a year or so later.

Riving shingles used to be known as "grandfather's favorite pastime" for it was a man's chore that could be done while sitting down.

> 17 : *Father and I took Daniel and the wagon to Mr. Beach's to collect our mill-wheel. It is beautiful. It weighs over two tons!*
> 18 : *We rolled the mill-wheel over the new bridge, which did not sag an inch!*

WORKING *in the* WOODSHED

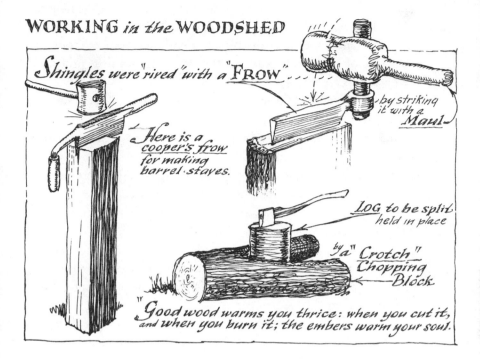

Shingles were "rived" with a "FROW".

by striking it with a Maul

Here is a cooper's frow for making barrel-staves.

LOG *to be split held in place*

by a "Crotch" *Chopping Block*

Good wood warms you thrice: when you cut it, and when you burn it; the embers warm your soul.

19 : Rog. Sunday. After meeting, we all walked our bound-aries. Met the Adams doing the same.

"Rog. Sunday" as Noah put it in his diary, meant Rogation Sunday, which was the day when farmers looked to their land and crops and prayed for a bountiful harvest. On this day, the clergyman and his flock walked through the village and out into the fields to bless the planted ground.

In the evening on Rogation Sunday, farmers and their families walked the boundaries of their property; it was both inventory and time for giving thanks for their land. At points along the way, some boy of the family group was "bumped" against a marker tree or a boundary stone, or he was ducked into whatever pond or stream marked the boundary.

33

It was all in good fun, and the bumping or ducking was accompanied by a small gift to the boy. In this way, he well remembered the boundaries of the land which he would some day fall heir to.

The Adams family met with the Blakes as both families were walking the boundaries of their land. Noah spotted the Adamses first, probably because he was so eager to see Sarah.

"Hi there!" he yelled. "Over here are some markers—I guess we are right on the line!"

"We've bumped Robert on two trees already," called out Mr. Adams. "Have you been bumped yet, Noah?"

Noah felt he was too old for such childish customs, but just to join in the fun, and perhaps to delight Sarah, he allowed himself to be bumped against a pile of marker stones. And it was Sarah who rewarded him with a package of sweet cookies.

After Rogationtide walk and before the sun had set, the Adams family went back with the Blakes to view the new mill-wheel.

"What a fine wheel!" exclaimed Mr. Adams. "It should give you extraordinary power."

"Yes," said Izaak, "It is an *overshot wheel* and they say that they are most efficient. With it we can keep the water power locked up in the mill-pond till we want to use it. Even when the stream ceases to flow, we can still have water for the mill. The first thing I shall attach to the wheel will be a bellows for the forge. Then perhaps a drop-hammer and a wood saw or maybe a device for grinding linseed oil."

"And what about a *gristmill?*" asked Rachel. "I am tired of buying meal from town or grinding it in my ancient quern."

"Yes," said Izaak, "your quern shall go to Indian Tom who has so often admired it. And I shall put in a small gristmill just for you!"

Everyone looked at the big wheel as it sat resting on the far end of the new bridge, and they imagined the wonderful things it would some day do. But to Izaak, who had to do most of the work, the stone foundations and the mill house with its final machinery, seemed a long way off.

But things were beginning to shape up. There was the new bridge for hauling materials across, there was a fine new water wheel ready to go

The QUERN *was a simple hand-mill.*

Grain was poured through a hole in the upper millstone, . . .

LOWER (STATIONARY) STONE

— ground against a lower stone, and thrown outward to fall as meal

Rachel swings the "Quern stick" to turn the upper mill stone

to work, there was the pond and there was the sluice box ready to lead water from the pond to the wheel.

As with all back-country places, the Blake homesite was near a spring of running water; a well had been made only after the house had been completed. By the year of Noah's diary, the old stream used both for washing and drinking water (marked "watering place" on the 1790 drawing) had been diverted into a pond and a real well had been dug. If you look at the second ("after 1805") drawing you will see the well and wellsweep at the upper right corner.

"We'll build the sweep," Izaak had said, "even before we have finished the well. And you'll probably want to know why. Well, the reason is simple. It will be an easy way to lift out the earth as I dig it away; that will be your job, Noah."

And so a crotched tree was found and a big spruce sweep was pinioned into the crotch; another spruce pole hung from the sweep tip, and a bucket was hung from that. The butt end of the pole was so heavy that it lifted the bucket up, even with water or earth in it. And it was always easier to pull that sweep *down* by your own natural weight than

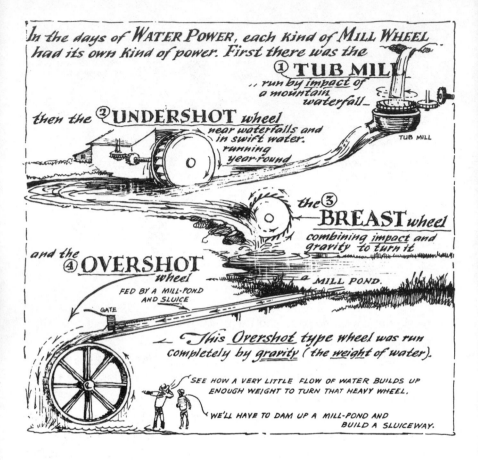

In the days of WATER POWER, each kind of MILL WHEEL had its own kind of power. First there was the

① TUB MILL
.. run by *impact* of a mountain waterfall_

TUB MILL

then the ② UNDERSHOT wheel
near waterfalls and in swift water. running year-round

the ③ BREAST wheel
combining impact and gravity to turn it

a MILL POND.

and the ④ OVERSHOT wheel
FED BY A MILL-POND AND SLUICE

GATE

This Overshot type wheel was run completely by gravity (the weight of water).

SEE HOW A VERY LITTLE FLOW OF WATER BUILDS UP ENOUGH WEIGHT TO TURN THAT HEAVY WHEEL.

WE'LL HAVE TO DAM UP A MILL-POND AND BUILD A SLUICEWAY.

it would be to pull the loaded bucket up, using your strength instead of your weight.

With the well finished, a pond became the new project. We might presume that building a pond took a year or two, but nature takes over quickly and within a short time after any pond is designed, you will find frogs and fish and weeds and water-snakes, all appearing miraculously and as if the pond had always been there.

Of course, the object of the pond was to eventually feed the mill-to-be and during off hours and rainy days, Izaak and Noah had worked on building the wooden sluice which would carry the pond water down to the mill and then by the water's weight, turn the wheel. It was the sluice box that first gave American designers the idea for the canal, for on some of the farms, men made wooden canal-like boxes with water in them and by floating long narrow boats in these "sluices," heavy loads could be carried easily from the barn to the road, from a mine to the smelter, or from the forest to the sawmill. By the 1800's, and just before the locomotive came into being, America had really become canal-minded and everything went from town to town by canal-boat. Even today we still say that we "ship" things from town to town although

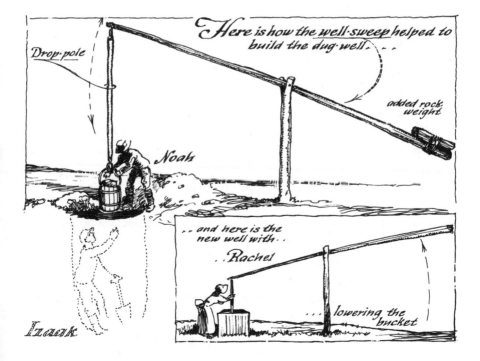

Drop-pole

Here is how the well-sweep helped to build the dug-well.

added rock weight

Noah

Izaak

.. and here is the new well with ..

.. Rachel

... lowering the bucket

Even farmers had their private little canals, for hauling heavy loads,

a sluice filled with water, a cargo-boat floating in it.

now it really goes by railroad or truck. And even now, if you look carefully, you will see evidence along many highways that there was once a canal. Most of our railroads were built along the tow-path of old canals where the mules once walked to pull canal boats: the actual canal (long since dry) will still be seen running along one side of the railroad tracks and still acting as a good drainage for rain water.

> *20 : Showers.*
> *21 : do.*
> *22 : do.*
> *23 : Father and Mr. Beach started on the mill (foundation).*
> *24 : I helped at the mill site. Began a plumping mill for Mother.*

"Mother," said Noah, "I've a surprise for you! Come down to the mill bank and see what I have begun. I know that Father promised to attach a grain mill to his water wheel for you, but I think I've beat him to it! I am making you a real plumping mill."

Rachel was eager to see Noah's invention; even as she neared the bank where her husband and Mr. Beach were hard at work with the dry-wall foundations, she could hear the steady sound of plumping. When she reached the bank, she saw it.

"It may be slow," explained Noah, "but it will work on and on all by itself. I guess it might pound out a full measure of meal in about half an hour. Father says when he gets his water wheel in place, I can use just the spray from it to make my mill work."

Using merely the overflow and leakage from the sluice, Noah's mill

38

had a little box that filled with water every now and then. When it filled, the added weight lifted a big hammer-like object at the other end. And as soon as this went up, the box emptied itself so the hammer lost balance and fell down into a hollowed mortar log with a resounding thud.

"It works fine," called out Izaak from the other bank. "I guess we have a pretty clever son. Takes after his father, all right!" he added with a chuckle.

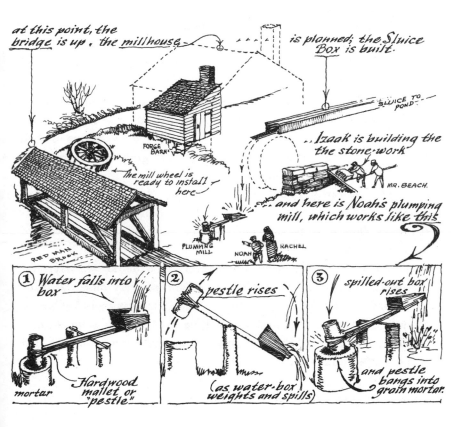

at this point, the bridge is up. the millhouse— is planned; the Sluice Box is built.

SLUICE TO POND

...Izaak is building the the stone work

the mill wheel is ready to install here

FORGE BARN

MR. BEACH.

...and here is Noah's plumping mill, which works like this

PLUMPING MILL

NOAH   RACHEL

RED MAN BROOK

① Water falls into box

mortar   Hardwood mallet or "pestle"

② pestle rises

(as water-box weights and spills)

③ spilled-out box rises

and pestle bangs into grain mortar.

"Izaak Blake, you can go right back to your mill-building," replied Rachel, with a twinkle in her eye. "You can saw wood, or grind linseed, or pump a bellows, or mix snuff with your old mill for all I care! Noah and I have our own mill! If you are real good and polite to us, we might just let you have some of our good cornmeal!"

Rachel knew how her husband had wanted for a long while to build himself a mill for sawing wood and to do other mechanical jobs. After all, she really didn't mind grinding the small amount of meal needed for a family of three, but still she must have been proud of her son's new invention.

"When I get it in place," said Noah, "I'll carve my initials and the date into it. And your initials too, Mother, for it shall be your mill."

In modern times when everything a person needs may be bought in a store, there are very few hand-made things left. So we are robbed of that rare and wonderful satisfaction that comes with personal accomplishment. In Noah's time, nearly every single thing a person touched was the result of his own efforts. The cloth of his clothing, the meal on the table, the chair he sat in, and the floor he walked upon, all were made by the user. This is why those people had an extraordinary awareness of life. They knew wood intimately; they knew the ingredients of food and medicines and inks and paints because *they* grew it and ground it and mixed it themselves. It was this awareness of everything about them that made the early American people so full of inner satisfaction, so grateful for life and all that went with it. Nowadays modern conveniences allow us to be forgetful, and we easily become less aware of the wonders of life.

We are apt to ponder why almost everything of the old days was initialed and dated. It was simply because almost everything was made by the one who initialed it; the date was added because everyone was so completely aware of the times in which he lived. Any boy would certainly put his name and the date on a mill he had designed himself, and Noah was no exception.

25 : Father and Mr. Beach at sawing.

40

26 : Rained all day. Set the saws with Father and later went fishing.

27 : I took Mr. Beach's place at the saw. He hurt his eye and is ill.

We might argue as to what kind of a saw Izaak and Mr. Beach used and what they were sawing, but it is most likely they were smooth-sawing timbers for the wheel and gear housing—that place where the water wheel would turn a wooden gear on the big axle. This gear would then mesh with a larger gear and become the machine for doing whatever work Izaak wanted it to do: In those days, big square beams were either broadaxed from round logs or they were sawed into a square shape with a pit-saw. Either the log being sawed was propped up so one of the sawyers could get under it, or the log was shoved across a pit in the ground with one man in the pit. In either case, the man on top had the more desirable job, for the man beneath was showered with sawdust at every stroke of the pit-saw. Perhaps Mr. Beach "hurt his eye" by getting sawdust into it which would indicate that he was "box-man" (or the man below) while Izaak worked from above as the "tiller-man."

All the first sawmills were "up-and-down sawmills" and the saw was like the framed pit-saw shown in the drawing; the frame slid up and down just as a window sash does in its framing. In fact, the saw was held in a "sash" and it slid up and down in a "frame," and with little doubt our modern wooden window was designed from the old up-and-down sawmill's sash and frame.

On the page opposite the pit-saw drawing, you will see how later on, the framed hand saw became mechanized. For a smaller saw, the workman's foot pushed the blade down and then it sprang back by itself by means of a springy sapling. An apprentice (helper-student) sometimes did this work for him. For rougher and heavier sawing, an apprentice turned a big wheel, or a horse entered the picture by working some kind of a treadmill, which in turn slid a saw back and forth, as the drawing shows.

28 : Fruit trees are in full blossom. Plowed today.

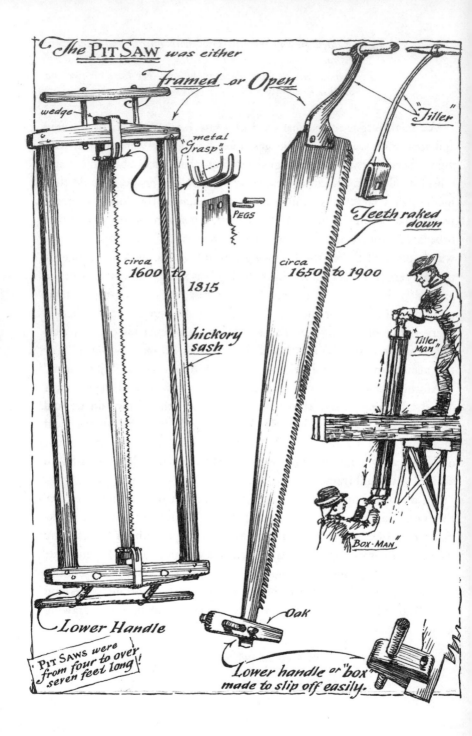

The PIT SAW was either *Framed* or *Open*

wedge

"metal Grasp"

PEGS

circa 1600 to 1815

hickory sash

Lower Handle

PIT SAWS were from four to over seven feet long!

"Tiller"

Teeth raked down

circa 1650 to 1900

Tiller Man

Box-Man

Oak

Lower handle or "box" made to slip off easily.

29 : Plowed.

30 : Rain set in again. Father is working under cover at the mill.

31 : Finished plowing. Signs of a few days of dry weather.

"Signs of a few days of dry weather" can be good news to any farmer who has been walking about in mud for a whole week. These weather "signs" were what the old-time farmer looked for in the sky, the di-

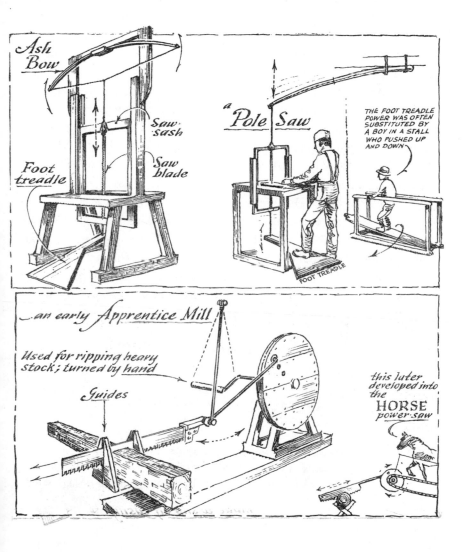

Ash Bow

Saw sash

Foot treadle

Saw blade

a "Pole Saw"

THE FOOT TREADLE POWER WAS OFTEN SUBSTITUTED BY A BOY IN A STALL WHO PUSHED UP AND DOWN

FOOT TREADLE

an early Apprentice Mill

Used for ripping heavy stock; turned by hand

Guides

this later developed into the HORSE power-saw

rection of the wind, and the disposition of his cattle. Today we go about our business regardless of rain or shine, but not so long ago what we did the next day depended entirely upon the weather. When roads were made of dirt, even the slightest rain often made carriage traffic out of the question. A round trip to town at five miles an hour might take all day, and part of the trip might even have to be made at night on dark roads, so people chose a time of month when the moon stayed fullest and the skies were clearest. Your almanac was your timetable.

People now look upon almanacs as silly superstitious writings that dealt with the moon in a mystic way and predicted what the weather would be, using witchcraft methods. Nothing could be more incorrect. Just as modern scientists use information about last year's storms and seasons, and feed that information to electronic calculator machines, so did the old-time farmer keep daily weather accounts of the past and add them up year after year. Farm diaries and almanacs were the books which kept such records.

Want to take your cattle on a three-day trip to the market? Just open your almanac and see when the moon is fullest to make your night travel possible. Did your clock stop and do you want to set it again? Just open your almanac and find out the minute of sunrise or sunset today. Want to start on a boat trip to deliver your grain? Consult your almanac and find out what hour tomorrow's tide will be highest.

And so it went; in the days when there were no telephones or even neighbors close by, your almanac was far from being a scrap-book of superstitions—it was an absolute necessity.

Noah's "signs of dry weather" might have been some of those listed in his almanacs and which you might want to remember:

Heavy dew at night means a fair dry day tomorrow.
Halo around sun or moon means a lengthy slow rain within eight hours.
Smoke refusing to rise signifies oncoming storm.
Increased odors of swamps, ditches, cellars, warns of rain.
Rolls of dark clouds under cobwebby sky warns of high wind.
Bats and swallows fly near the ground before a rain.

Chapter 5

1 : First day of June! Earliest sunrise this month.
2 : Whitsunday. Worked on garden which is entirely up.
Was real hoe-boy.

Here you might wonder, for knowing how religious the early American was, and remembering how even stagecoaches stopped running on the Sabbath, doesn't it seem odd that Noah "worked on the garden" during Sunday? The answer is likely that he worked *after sundown*, for at that time the Sabbath began on Saturday at sundown and ended on Sunday at sundown. In fact, the old "Saturday night bath" started from the adage about cleanliness being akin to Godliness. So we might assume that Noah worked in the garden as Sunday night drew on.

It is interesting to note here how farmers used to work in what we now call darkness. Many present-day scientists insist that the early countryman had extraordinary eyesight, keener than the average eyesight of today. Farmers frequently did their haying at night, using the moon or the stars for illumination, and taking advantage of the coolness of summer night. At any rate, it seems remarkable that so much work did get done with so few mechanical conveniences and without the use of outdoor lanterns. Many farms had no lanterns and those that did used them more for carrying a flame from place to place than for actual illumination.

The most common farm lantern was the metal one, punched with many holes. Glass lanterns are most rare. The drawing also shows a simple tin measuring can with holes punched through it for carrying a candle.

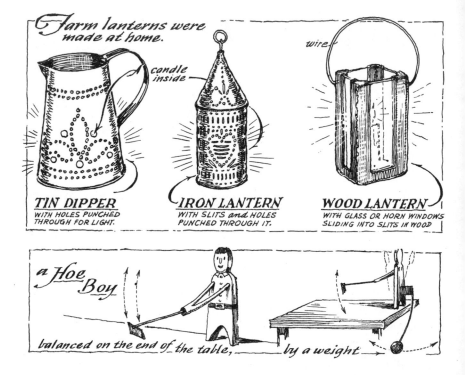

Farm lanterns were made at home.

candle inside

wire

TIN DIPPER
WITH HOLES PUNCHED THROUGH FOR LIGHT.

IRON LANTERN
WITH SLITS *and* HOLES PUNCHED THROUGH IT.

WOOD LANTERN
WITH GLASS OR HORN WINDOWS SLIDING INTO SLITS IN WOOD

a Hoe Boy

balanced on the end of the table,   by a weight

Below the lantern drawings you may see the author's explanation of what Noah might have meant when he wrote in his diary, ". . . was real hoe-boy." A popular toy of the early 1800's was a balancing figure that sat on the end of a table and moved up and down for a great while. First it was a man riding a horse; but then there was a very popular song called "The Hoe Boy," and the toy took on the form of the boy with a hoe, who once started, went up and down with his little hoe. Several hoe-boy toys have been found in New England.

> *3 : Helped Father build rope hoist to move the water wheel.*
> *4 : Father and Mr. Adams worked at putting the water wheel in place. Sarah did not come.*
> *5 : Tried the wheel: it is quite true and has great force. Father will begin fashioning the cog wheel.*
> *6 : Cut grass until rain started. First hay of the year.*
> *7 : Mowed.*
> *8 : do.*
> *9 : Sunday. Saw Sarah and she promised to visit me at mowing.*
> *10 : Rain. Sarah did not come. Will use half the hay for bedding and half for the pit.*

It almost takes a detective to decide what Noah might have meant by using half the hay "for the pit." This must have been the early version of the modern farm silo, for believe it or not, the first silos were pits in the ground! The word silo cannot be found in the early American dictionary; it comes from the French, meaning a hole or pit. And in the beginning of our farm life, people stored cattle food in the ground instead of in those towering round buildings we are now so familiar with.

As you travel across the countryside, you might notice how most of the old farm silos are leaning. The reason for this is that, unlike old barns that have big beam framework, the silo has no such skeleton—it is all skin and suffers from poor design. If the early farmers had designed them, they would probably have big beams and they would not lean. Noticing such things makes a detective of the historian and tells us how architecture changes from time to time.

SILO.. the building that is all skin ⌐ and wants to lean.
.. Noah's storage silo was a hole
in the ground
← Corn and Hay

11 : I am to do all the farm work. Father shall work full time on the mill.

12 : Mr. Beach is fitting the mill machinery while Father frames the mill house. I have never been so tired from farm chores!

For a young boy to have taken over the farm chores in mid-June certainly must have been a tiresome bit of work. But in those days people did not farm to raise saleable crops; they farmed for their own table and for their own livestock.

Noah and his father seldom saw each other except at mealtime, each one working so hard at his own chores; Rachel managed to hear the progress report then.

"Goodness!" remarked Rachel to her husband, "I don't see why your mill house must be so much better built than our own home. Why those timbers you are using for framing are big enough to support a herd of elephants!"

"When the mill begins to operate," said Izaak, "you'll think there *is* a herd of elephants within the mill. I guess you've never been in a mill house."

Rachel hadn't, or she would have known how a water wheel will make the whole mill structure shudder and weave with its tremendous power. Just as a modern man might enjoy the power and noise of a sports automobile, or any mechanical device, the old-time miller derived

48

great satisfaction from the enormous energy that turned the wheel and operated many tons of massive gears. It is the sort of job a man becomes wedded to.

The drawing of house framing might appear technical and boring to the reader at first, but when you inspect it closely and see how the whole house frame went up without even one nail, each piece locking into another and holding itself fast, one can only marvel at the early craftsmanship. Nowadays people build merely to get the house up and to live in it or to sell it. Once people created buildings for themselves and their children's children. They enjoyed looking at the beams that made a castle of a farmhouse, withstanding the ages; and they derived the greatest pleasure from perfection of craftsmanship.

Looking at the old-time workmanship, the modern builder will always remark, "You couldn't afford to do that today," or "They had all the time in the world then." Both statements are so untrue! We are richer now than ever. And as for having more time in the old days, the lack of mechanical time-savers made the early American's work day about three times as long as our present day.

> 13 : *Robert Adams came by; said his family are coming Saturday to see the new mill house. It is all framed. Sarah will be here on Saturday!*
> 14 : *Finished plowing and planting too; helped Father make tidy around the mill.*
> 15 : *All the Adams arrived. Sarah and I took lunch upstream to see the beavers and Sarah cut her foot in wading. I carried her all the way back.*
> 16 : *Sunday. Sarah not at Meeting. Her foot bled.*

Here we might wonder if the cut on Sarah's foot reopened and so bled again, or if a doctor had "bled" her. For even in 1805 (and indeed much later) the custom of bleeding was resorted to in almost every serious ailment. George Washington, whose death had occurred only six years before in 1799, probably died from his doctor's "remedy" of bleeding rather than from his ailment, which was only a sore throat!

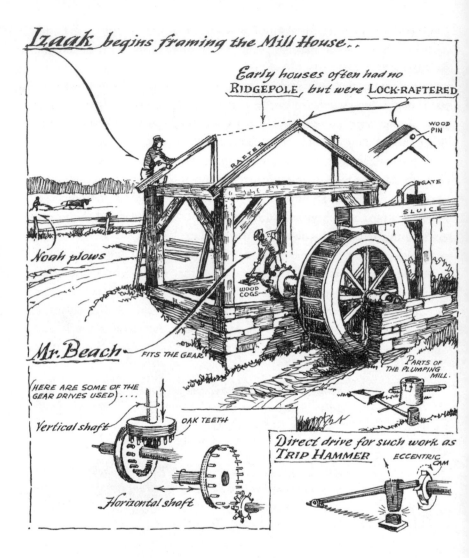

Izaak begins framing the Mill House...

Early houses often had no RIDGEPOLE, but were LOCK-RAFTERED

WOOD PIN

RAFTER

GATE

SLUICE

Noah plows

WOOD COGS

Mr. Beach FITS THE GEAR

PARTS OF THE PLUMPING MILL

(HERE ARE SOME OF THE GEAR DRIVES USED)....

Vertical shaft

OAK TEETH

Direct drive for such work as TRIP HAMMER

ECCENTRIC CAM

Horizontal shaft

17 : Alarm of frost last night but no thing was harm'd. In spite of the coolness, I saw several humming birds and humble-bees in the garden.

Here again the author was puzzled by the wording in Noah's diary.

Did Noah mean *bumblebees?* Oddly enough, however, we find that none of the early dictionaries have any mention of *bumblebee*, but they all do list *humblebee!* The early Quakers were called "the humble people" because they refused to fight or kill; the humblebee was so called because it was thought that it, too, did not fight or sting. How the name finally became bumblebee is strange, except that it certainly does look more "bumble" than "humble."

Plate

Girt

Flare
from
about
1 to 3 inches.
(exagerrated here)

Corner Post

F L O O R

Wedged
tenon

FRONT SILL

END SILL

Sills held together by weight of house, not by pegs.

Cellar Framework of a typical wooden Farm House of 1800's

The Cellar SUMMER *beam* carried the JOISTS for the first floor.
(often logs <u>round</u> beneath and <u>flat</u> on top).
bark often left intact.

Chimney

Corner post mortise

END SILL

Front SILL

Cellar Chimney GIRTS

18 : *Father still working at the mill. Mr. Beach stayed with us.*

19 : *The mill wheel has been set and there will be several diversions (evidently this meant several machines harnessed to the same power). Father and Mr. Beach making use of the longest days of the year. Cogs will work both a hammer and the bellows, so some of my forge work shall be eliminated. It is all very wonderful.*

20 : *Rain stopped all work at the mill. I worked at farming.*

21 : *do.*

22 : *Went to see Sarah this night, bringing some wild honeysuckle. She was much better and might go to Meeting tomorrow.*

23 : *Sarah was at Meeting. She wore a sprig of my honeysuckle, which had become very brown'd. The weather is warm and the days have become beautiful.*

Certainly the days are beautiful when your best girl remembers to wear a bit of your bouquet to her!

But Noah's mind must have also been filled with the wonders of his father's new mill machinery. The magic of water power did so many things that before were drudgery, that adding some new device was as thrilling as our buying a new TV or washing machine for our home today. Some millers, so the records say, even attached a cord to the big wheel to rock the baby's cradle or to turn a spit in the fireplace and revolve the roast.

24 : *Worked in the garden today and pruned in the orchard. Found many of the apple and pear trees with insects.*

25 : *Cleaned the chimneys at the forge barn and in the house and sooted about the trees. First dish of pease from the garden!*

26 : *Father and I sledded the oaks from the woodlot and put them down near the mill.*

"It won't be long now, son," said Izaak, "before we can saw these oak logs into flooring for the house. And with our own saw!"

"You mean you will have the machinery set up before winter?" asked Noah.

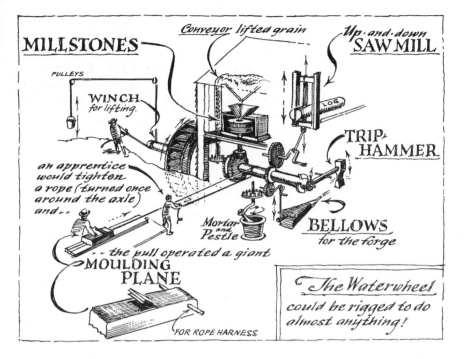

MILLSTONES

Conveyor lifted grain

Up·and·down
SAW MILL

PULLEYS

WINCH
for lifting.

an apprentice
would tighten
a rope (turned once
around the axle)
and ··

TRIP·
HAMMER

Mortar
and
Pestle

BELLOWS
for the forge

·· the pull operated a giant
MOULDING
PLANE

FOR ROPE HARNESS

The Waterwheel
could be rigged to do
almost anything!

"Mr. Beach is in town working on the saw-frame this very minute. But there's a lot of timber work to be cut and placed before we can set up the sawmill."

The thought of their own sawmill, and logs being cut into fine new planks, made Noah's work easier as he jacked the oaks up a skid and onto the sled. Sleds were used as much in summer as they were in winter at that time, for wheels were all but useless in heavy hauling across the old unimproved trails. And Daniel, who was used to pulling a sled, knew just how to push his great weight against the sled first, to jounce it loose from the earth, and then begin the slow pull across the grass and soft mud.

But Daniel was different today. He seemed slow and more attentive to Noah than he did to his work at logging. He nosed about Noah's

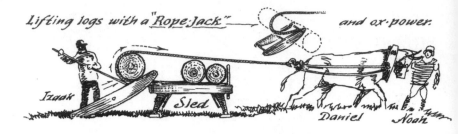

Lifting logs with a "Rope-Jack" and ox-power.

Izaak

Sled

Daniel   Noah

clothes as if looking for salt and he swung his head up and down quickly in the manner that he always did when Noah came to the barn first thing in the morning.

"Come on Daniel," said Noah, "It's not morning now—it's time for work! Put your back into it and heave ho!"

Izaak was guiding the logs up and into the sled, using a long bar, but he couldn't help noticing there was something different about Daniel today.

27 : Thursday. This has been a poor day. Daniel is dead.

When Noah had gone to the barn that morning, he noticed Bessie at the door. It had always been Daniel who came to greet him first. Bessie had called with her usual low moo the instant she saw Noah coming, but there was no sign of Daniel.

When Noah reached the barn he saw Daniel lying in the hay. His eyes were open, but they were not focused on anything. It was clear that Daniel was dead.

Noah went inside and sat on the big body, which was still warm and soft. He must have been there for some time, and he must have remembered all the work and good times that he had lived through with Daniel. The big animal had become a part of the household, for he had helped to build it. He had helped to build the new bridge, even to pull the first logs for the old bridge. All the clearing and plowing was his work.

After a long while Noah felt the body beneath him growing stiff and cold. He rose slowly and opened the door to let Bessie out. But for the first time, the old cow stood still and refused to leave the barn. Noah walked toward the house as if he were dragging all the weight that Daniel had pulled over those fields. It would be difficult to break the news.

> 28 : *We buried Daniel. Father says we shall have a horse.*
> 29 : *Mother layed out her flower garden today. I finished sooting the orchard trees.*
> 30 : *Sunday. I told Sarah about Daniel. We shall plant a fine tree over his grave.*

Along with the old diary, there were several papers folded and inserted within the leather cover; one was a recipe "to destroy Insects on Fruit trees." It read:

> Take 2 shovelsfull of soot, one of Quick Lime; mixed together; take some of this and put it windward of the tree, and sprinkle some water upon it, when a great quantity of Gas will be evolved, which ascending into the Tree will destroy Insects, without injury to the Plant, as it rather helps Vegetable life.

The reader might enjoy the fine use and rhythm of language in this simple direction which was probably written by a plain farmer. Without knowing who did the writing, but knowing that this is probably what Noah followed when he "sooted the orchard trees," we herewith reproduce the actual writing:

Chapter 6

1 : July. The Adams and we are going to spend the Independence Day in the village to see the holyday fun. Father hopes to buy a horse on that day.

"Holyday" was first thought by the author to be a misspelling by Noah, but on searching through dictionaries of Noah's time, there was no word *holiday*; there was *holyday* instead, meaning exactly what our holiday now means.

2 : Thunder shower before sunrise. I dug new potatoes.
3 : More rain. It cleared tonight, and tomorrow should be clear for our going to town.
4 : Never heard so many bells and cannon shots. Several wagonloads were on their way as we walked to the village. Last year poor Daniel drove us in. Mr. Adams was reading the Declaration of Independence when we arrived

and Mr. Grimes said a long prayer. Sarah looked very pretty. Father bought a horse and a waggon! We shall collect them on Saturday.

"Here," cried the auctioneer, "is as fine a beast as any man would want! And with her goes an almost new wagon! Surely I can get one higher bid—who will raise it another five dollars?"

Just then someone in the crowd with a little cannon lit the fuse and held his ears. Bang! The cannon exploded only a few feet behind Izaak, and his two hands went over his head as if he were shot.

"Thank you, Izaak Blake!" said the auctioneer. "There's a man who knows what he wants. One hand was enough but he put up two! Sold to Mr. Blake!"

Izaak almost protested. In fact he had already begun—but he did admire the horse, and the old farm wagon that Daniel had pulled for so long had already rotted in many places. He walked to the auction table to pay.

"Well," said Izaak later on, "we have a new horse and he came to us by fate and because of a toy cannon. I don't know what they called him before, but I have a name for him now. It shall be *Bang.*"

5 : We began making ready for Bang. Father says a horse will jump over such fences as ours so we began making them higher.

Noah and his father worked all the day carrying stone to heighten the stone fences.

"I sure miss Daniel," said Izaak as he struggled with a wheelbarrow of stones. "He could have slid this load and another ton as if it were nothing. But when I was a boy, we didn't have wheelbarrows! We had only handbarrows; some of them had long handles, and we slid the load behind us just as an Indian does with a travois."

"Mother will have a hard time climbing over the fence if we make it so high," observed Noah. "Shouldn't we make a little ladder for her—or one of those things called a *stile?*"

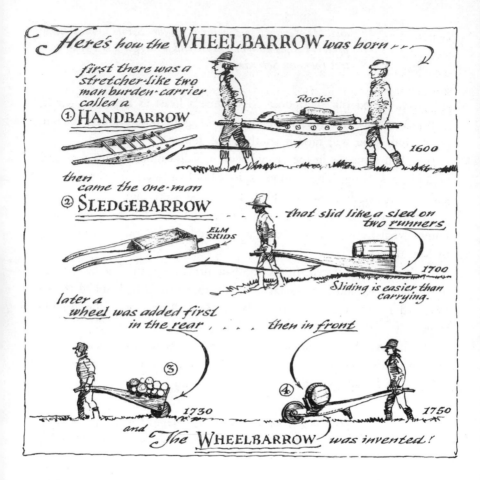

"Perhaps we can put a grike here and there," replied Izaak. "These are slits in a fence where a person can pass over, but a farm animal would be too timid to squeeze through. I do admit grikes are more for men and boys than they are for ladies with flowing skirts, so perhaps we shall build a stile for Mother."

In 1805 wire was not yet used in fence work (barbed wire was invented in 1873), but wood was so plentiful in America that two or three men could split rails and build a fence with them at close to a mile per week. Between the stone walls made just from land clearing and the stump fences resulting from the same work, there wasn't much more fence work to be done at the Blake place, except to heighten a wall here and there or to add a rail on top of the lower stumps. So before the day was over, there was good enclosure for Bang—high enough to keep the average horse from jumping over.

It is interesting to the student of early times to note that fence rails were cut (by law in some places) at a length of eleven feet. This was exactly one sixth of that old measuring device, the *chain*, which was a linked measure sixty-six feet long used by surveyors instead of the foot and inch calculation that we use now. By merely walking around your

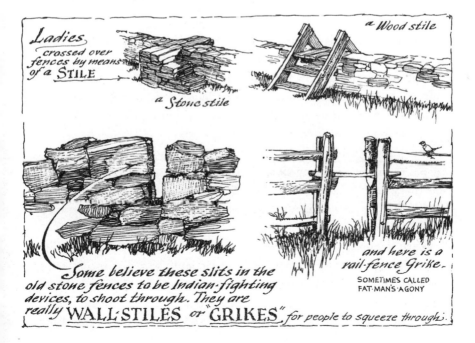

Ladies crossed over fences by means of a STILE →

a Wood stile

a Stone stile

Some believe these slits in the old stone fences to be Indian-fighting devices, to shoot through. They are really WALL-STILES or "GRIKES", for people to squeeze through.

and here is a rail-fence Grike.
SOMETIMES CALLED FAT-MAN'S-AGONY

fence line and counting the fence rails, you could accurately tell the size of your land. Or by removing a rail, you could use that as a giant ruler for measuring out more land. Lay out two rails and you would have the legal width of a roadway where Noah lived. Yes, in those days there were many good reasons for custom, and the people enjoyed tradition because they knew the reason for it.

> 6 : *A most exciting Saturday. We went to the village to col-*
> *lect Bang and the waggon. Bang is faster on the road than*
> *Daniel; we arrived home in less than ten minutes. Bessie*
> *would have none of Bang and she kicked her stall through.*
> *We shall leave Bang at pasture until the two animals be-*
> *come better friends.*
> 7 : *Went to Meeting in the new waggon. It is great enjoy-*
> *ment to drive a horse.*
> 8 : *Brilliant warm day. Father and Mr. Beach squared new*
> *timbers for the mill machinery. I tried my hand at the*
> *squaring axe while Father and Mr. Beach chizelled.*

Any man who was expert at using a broadaxe (a squaring axe), had usually learned the hard way and had the marks on his legs to show it. For the broadaxe wasn't a thing to cut down trees with, but a sort of giant plane that chipped away at round logs to make them square. Its handle was short and its blades were razor sharp; you had to be "on your toes every second or the broadaxe would."

The drawing shows an adze, cutting measured notches while a broad-axe did the actual chopping away, but very often there was no adze used and the whole process was axe work. So most of the "antique adzed beams" that we see nowadays were never even touched by an adze; they were broadaxed instead.

When it came to the mortices and tenons (the interlocking units that joined timbers together), a combination axe and chisel was used (as the drawing shows). Almost none of these tools are left, as they were re-placed in the early 1800's by the straight chisel, but we might assume that Izaak and Mr. Beach used this sort of thing when they "chizelled" as the diary relates.

60

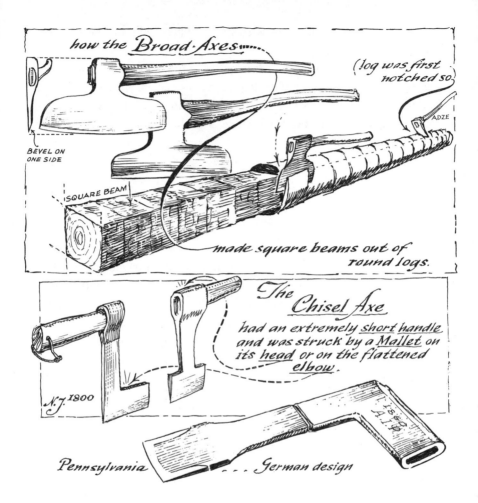

how the *Broad·Axes*

(log was first notched so)

ADZE

BEVEL ON ONE SIDE

SQUARE BEAM

made square beams out of round logs.

The Chisel Axe had an extremely <u>short handle</u> and was struck by a <u>Mallet</u> on its <u>head</u> or on the flattened <u>elbow</u>.

N.J. 1800

Pennsylvania . . . German design

"Well," said Izaak, "your work at the bellows is now past history! We have finally made a cog in the water wheel axle that should lift up the bellows twice with every revolution. Pretty soon we can dismantle the old forge barn and set it up in the new mill house."

"That's one job I'll never miss," laughed Noah, "but I'm sure you'll find another job for me, just as tiresome. There will still be nail hammering to do."

"The way things look," said Izaak, "we may not be making nails at all before long. A fellow in Philadelphia has come up with a remarkable nail machine, and I've already seen what it can do. They had a keg of machine-made nails in the town store, and they looked pretty good to me. But there will always be a market for good iron tools, and that's what we're going to make in our mill!"

> *9 : Father says we shall make iron hoes and shovels and dogs in the new mill; there will be a cutter for bar iron.*

Dogs? A lot of things were called dogs in the early days, but Izaak probably meant the things that men used to fasten a log with when it was squared or otherwise worked upon. It would seem to be natural to progress from nail-making to forging staple-dogs which are like large sized double nails, anyway. (It is interesting to note that although these timber dogs were in every household a century or so ago, they have become one of the rarest of tools; the author has only two in his collection.)

> *10 : Helped Mother with her sallet garden. Planted Rosemary and saffron and lettice and gilly-flowers. (Sallet was the old way of spelling salad, just as lettuce was spelled lettice.)*
>
> *11 : The brook is low, so we took advantage and built up the stonework. Bang drew his first load of stone by sled, but it was difficult.*
>
> *12 : Two Indians came by from the mountains on their way to the village. We fed them. They marvelled at our new bridge.*
>
> *13 : Rain all the day.*
>
> *14 : Sarah drove back with us from Meeting and had Sunday night dinner with us. Mr. Adams collected and took her home in the evening.*

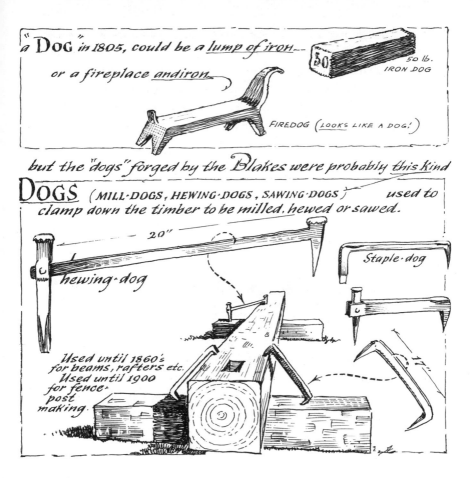

"a Dog" in 1805, could be a lump of iron—

or a fireplace andiron

50 lb. IRON DOG

FIREDOG (LOOKS LIKE A DOG!)

but the "dogs" forged by the Blakes were probably this kind

DOGS (MILL-DOGS, HEWING-DOGS, SAWING-DOGS) used to clamp down the timber to be milled, hewed or sawed.

20"

hewing-dog

Staple-dog

Used until 1860's for beams, rafters etc. Used until 1900 for fence-post making.

15 : Mr. Adams came by this morning to warn us of Indians. The same two that visited with us, followed them all the way home last night and would not reply when addressed. Perhaps they had been drinking. We shall draw our shutters at night.

16 : Good haying weather. Father and I worked in the field and we began building a rick.

Most people living today have never seen a real old-time haystack, or as they called it in the early days, a *rick*. Often hay ricks were square, but the usual kind was round and curving outward at the top like an inverted bell to ward off the downpour of rain. Ricks were not just piles of hay, but were built carefully with each sheaf folded neatly into place. They were constructed with all the finesse of an expert brickmason.

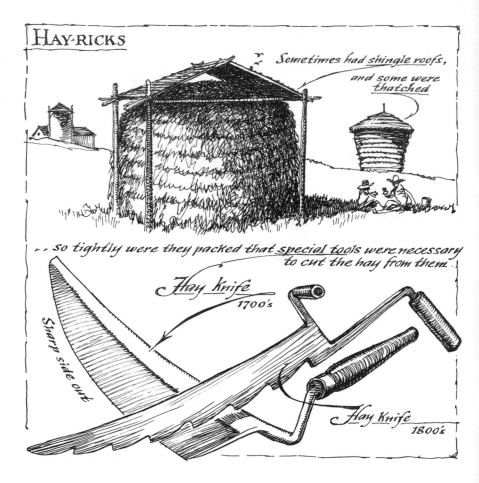

HAY·RICKS

Sometimes had shingle roofs, and some were thatched

..so tightly were they packed that special tools were necessary to cut the hay from them.

Hay Knife
1700's

Sharp side out

Hay Knife
1800's

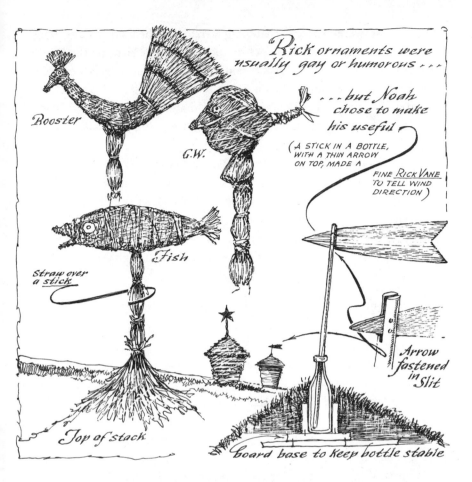

Rick ornaments were usually gay or humorous...

...but Noah chose to make his useful

(A STICK IN A BOTTLE, WITH A THIN ARROW ON TOP, MADE A FINE *RICK VANE* TO TELL WIND DIRECTION)

Rooster

G.W.

Fish

Straw over a stick

Arrow fastened in slit

Top of stack

board base to keep bottle stable

Even the strongest winds seldom toppled a good rick. During hot weather it was the greatest pleasure to noon and lunch in its shade while the sweet smell of hay perfumed the air on the lee side.

In America it usually was the custom to place an adjustable shingle roof atop a hay rick, but those farmers who leaned toward the old European ways thatched the top and peaked it with a gay straw ornament.

Those who were expert at thatching would use their rainy days designing rick ornaments in the shapes of roosters, fish, a boat, or the head of some well-known statesman. Of course, the event of a "rick-crowning" always called for drinks and song, but during harvest festivals each farm tried to outdo the other in the same spirit that we decorate our doorways during Christmas; then the ricks all over the countryside looked like big fancy holiday cakes.

Noah had seen one rick-top ornament that he wanted to duplicate and he decided to start making it as soon as the stacking got under way. It was a *rick vane*, made with a bottle with a short stick in it that held an arrow that swung and pointed into the wind. It seemed about the simplest way that anyone could build a weathervane, for the slick glass made a permanent and workable bearing for the upright stick.

17 : Rick is under way. Mr. Adams is going to thatch the roof for us. Carried water to Mother's garden which is dry.

Carrying water was always an important chore in the early days, for piping was almost unknown. As two buckets were as easy to carry as one, because of the counterbalance of weight, every household had one or more "neck yokes" or burden carriers. In fact they were made to fit each person's neck, so that a man's yoke was much different from that of a child or a woman, and in New York State, where they were made commercially, they had sizes from one to six, like shirts.

One favorite American burden carrier was made quickly from a square piece of canvas or waterproofed sailcloth, known in New England as a "summer cloth," which folded into a knapsack. Apples or grain could be carried in a summer cloth, but so could water or milk. The word summer had nothing to do with the season, but stemmed from the ancient word *sumpter* meaning *burden* or *burden-horse*. (The same applies to that main ceiling beam in the old houses known as a summer beam.)

Farmers in the north country still keep a square piece of waxed sailcloth in their wagons to carry water for their horses, for a bucket will

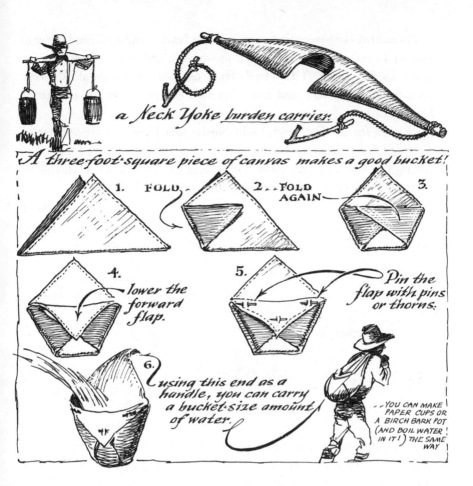

a Neck Yoke burden carrier

A three-foot-square piece of canvas makes a good bucket!

1. FOLD

2. FOLD AGAIN

3.

4. lower the forward flap.

5. Pin the flap with pins or thorns.

6. using this end as a handle, you can carry a bucket-size amount of water.

--YOU CAN MAKE PAPER CUPS OR A BIRCH BARK POT (AND BOIL WATER IN IT!) THE SAME WAY

dry out and leak, but a canvas bucket will always hold water. The drawing shows how to fold a summer cloth; in place of pins a plain thorn from a thorn tree will do the job of fastening the material. Indians have been known to make such an arrangement of birchbark, which will not burn as long as there is liquid on the inside, and will boil water over an open fire!

"Now that we have a new wagon," said Izaak, "and a spirited horse to pull it, I don't see why we can't also have a little two-wheel cart for going to the village. The wheels from our old wagon should do very well for building this, and the other two wheels might make a handy logging cart."

"I'm all for the little cart," said Noah, "but what is a *logging cart?*"

"Well," said Izaak to his son, "now that we are looking forward to having our own sawmill, there will be logs to move about, even to haul in from the woodlot, and Daniel isn't here to sled them. Bang would never get used to a logging sled, so we'll have to use wheels. A logging cart is nothing but two wheels between a long shaft: the log is jacked up to the axle and it can then be slid from place to place."

a LOGGING CART

So as time went on, the old Blake wagon began to disappear. First the rear wheels were dismantled to make the logging cart and then Noah was given the work of removing the bolts for use in a new cart body. Bolts and nails were not things to be discarded in the early days, and houses were often burned just to get the nails from them.

The right woods would have to be found for the new cart, for the wrong wood in any vehicle was unforgiveable. It was oak for the framework, elm for the sides and floor, ash for the spokes and shafts, pine for the seat, and hickory for the slats. Even a simple chair sometimes had as many as six kinds of wood, each kind working against the other in dry weather or damp, designed to stay tight and not to wear away or break. This is why an old wagon could sit outside year round in the weather and still exist, while a metal vehicle would rust and crumble. An automobile wheel left outside for twenty years would almost entirely disappear, yet you may see a two-hundred-year-old spinning wheel, sitting in the weather as they do outside many an antique shop, just about as good and useable as when it was made. It gives a thinking person food for thought, and to many of us a reverence for wood.

18 : We collected our first toll over the new bridge! A waggon crossed over, carrying a chapman and his wife.

"Father!" cried Noah, "There is a big wagon at our bridge!" Izaak came running and soon he and Noah were exchanging greetings with the driver, who had gotten down from a large covered wagon painted blue and filled with wares to sell. The sides were made like chests of boxes, each little door opening into a store of different articles, and each door with a title upon it.

The sides of the wagon were like chests of boxes...

"I see that you intend to roof over your bridge," said the man. "Good idea! A lot of people are planning to do that. I presume you ask a toll, but I see no sign."

"Well," said Izaak, "we just haven't come around to that yet. In fact, you are the first strangers to cross over. I shall be glad to give you free passing and our blessings."

NOAH·BLAKE·BRIDGE

Please walk your horse!

Foot passengers . . . . 1 cent
Horned cattle. . . . . 3 do.
Horse, Jack *or* Mule . . . . 3 do.
4 wheel carriage . . . . 10 do.
Burden cart *or* waggon . . . . 6 do.
Sleds *or* sleighs. . . . . 6 do.

Business with mill . . . nothing.
Sabbath day passage . . . do.

1805

PLEASE RING

Probable toll list and toll house arrangement

70

"Not on your life!" cried the man. "That would be bad luck to your bridge. Accept the toll and keep it for luck."

"If you insist," said Izaak, "but we had in mind asking ten cents for all four-wheel carriages. You see, we hope a stagecoach might use this road soon. Customers to our mill, when we get it in operation, will not be charged any toll."

"It is my pleasure," said the man, as he turned toward his wife, up on the wagon seat, who had fished the money from her bag and was handing it to him. "In fact, this is such an event, I would like to present you with a small gift. Do give these nutmegs to your good wife, whom I see looking down from the house."

He reached into his coat and came up with a handful of nutmegs.

The diary referred to this man as "a chapman" because 1805 was before the days of the Yankee peddler, and traveling merchants were known as *chapmen* (or more often, *petty chapmen*). These men sold almost everything, but they became known for their nutmegs, which were a small item and easy to carry. Connecticut specialized in outfitting traveling peddlers, so since the wares were known to come from that state, most people thought of all peddlers as coming from there, too. It was the peddler and his practice of carrying nutmegs that eventually gave Connecticut the name of "The Nutmeg State."

"Thank you," said Izaak as he accepted the nutmegs, "My wife is just out of such seasoning. Now I wonder if you might have a supply of salt in your stores?"

"Indeed I have!" said the chapman. "And the very best it is. I have a shipment of sea salt from the Jersey shore at two dollars a quarter bushel."

"We've been using mined salt here," said Izaak, "but I'd like to try the sea salt. They say it is difficult to manufacture."

"It is a complicated procedure and it takes a week or two to get the salt from sea water, but the Jersey coast is already dotted with windmills that pump the water up into shallow vats. Some men just let the sun do the work, while others boil the water down over a fire. Every hundred pounds of sea water, they say, has three and a half pounds of salt in it."

"I think you shall sell some of your salt in the village," Izaak ventured, "for I am sure they have none of it at the store."

Later, as the chapman drove off in the direction of the village, the new bridge looked much more important to Izaak and Noah.

"What shall I do with this money?" asked Noah.

"Well, the bridge is called Noah Blake Bridge, and I think Noah Blake should keep the money. But you shall have to keep proper account books."

Keeping an account book in 1805 demanded an extraordinary mathematical knowledge because English money was still in use here and there, while the currency from one state seldom was worth the same in another state. Here the author offers the reader an original page folded into the Noah Blake diary; it was evidently written by Izaak for his son Noah. The exact date is not known, but it shows the immense difficulty of ascertaining what our money was worth. Notice, too, the last line, which lists the New England group of states, and that Maine and Vermont are not yet among them.

> *19 : Worked in the fields. The corn is much too dry.*
> *20 : Mrs. Adams and Sarah went berrying and visited us. They reported seeing a bear among the berry bushes, so I accompanied them home where they showed me how they make blackberry wine.*

An early nineteenth-century recipe for blackberry wine was found by the author of this book; it seems very simple to make. It had the amusing title: "a medicinal drink for summer affections," and it read as follows:

> To a gallon of smashed blackberries, add a quart of boiling water and let this stand for a full day. Strain through a coarse cloth and add three quarts of water with two pounds of good brown sugar. Mix and put in a jug or keg, closing only partially by leaving the cork loose. Leaving this in a cool place, it should be ready for drinking in October.

21 : A sour, foggy Sunday.

22 : Heavy downpour, but good for the crops.
23 : Second day of rain. Father went to work under cover at the mill.
24 : Clear day. Worked in the fields. Some of the corn has washed away.
25 : Beginning of Dog Days. The Sun with Sirius now increases the heat.

A Table

Exhibiting the value of a Dollar in each of the United States and practical Theorems for exchangeing the currency of either into that of any other

To exchange from / to	N. Engl States & Virginia	Pennsylva Per-Delaw & Maryland	New York and N. Carolina	S. Carolina and Georgia
* New England States and Virginia	Dollar 6/0	Add one 4th	Add one 3d.	Subtract 1/3 twice
Pennsylvania N Jersey Delaware and Maryland	Subtract one 5th	Dollars 7/6	Add one 15th	X 3 1/7 8 ÷ 5
New York and North Caroline	Subtract one 4th	Subtract one 16th	Dollar 8/0	Do 2 add 1/6 of the 1/4
South Carolina and Georgia	Add two 7ths	Add 1/4 that 1/4 & 1/4 that 1/7	X 28 Sublt 1/7 Product	Dollar 4/8

*The New England States are New Hampshire Massachusets Rhode Island and Connecticut.

Many people now believe that the "dog days" of summer has something to do with the way the heat affects a dog; some say it is when most dogs go mad. But in the early days, when people were more generally educated in the science of the stars and planets, everyone knew the true meaning of the dog days. It is when Sirius, the Dog Star, brightest of stars, rises in conjunction with the sun. Some readers might argue with the author in saying that people were better educated over a century ago than they may be now in this age of space flight. Yet it is true that almost every farmer knew the stars and the complete routes and time-tables of the sun and the moon. The 1805 almanac for example, gave one full page to "the coming six eclipses of the year." Although five of the eclipses were invisible in America (because of time of day or location), the complete program of the visible eclipse was printed, down to the hour and minute and second of the beginning, immersion, middle eclipse, and so on. (The duration, incidentally, was 2 hours, 37 minutes, and 5 seconds.)

It is not that such information is no longer known or that we have not progressed immensely in our knowledge; the pertinent fact is that the average person doesn't know such things because they are not necessary information. A child today might say, "Why would I want to know if there is an eclipse unless I may see it?" But Benjamin Franklin observed that "knowing only what is necessary, makes living dull and marks the regression of learning." Noah couldn't see it, for it occurred on the opposite side of the earth, yet he shows more interest than the average schoolboy of today, when he puts in his diary:

> 26 : *Sun's eclipse at 25 minutes past one in the morning.*
> 27 : *Father is plumbing a fine new door for the mill house.*

"Plumbing" did not mean what it would mean today; because *plumb* was the word for *lead*, and a plumber was a man who worked with lead. Because all the first metal pipes were made from folded lead, the water-pipe makers became known as lead men or "plumbers." Noah's father did his "plumbing" with a piece of lead on a string, to get his doorframe absolutely vertical. Nowadays, of course, a carpenter would use a spirit level which employs a bubble in a vial of spirits (alcohol). In Noah's time there was probably no builder's level other than a gravity level, such as is shown in the drawing. The square model with the weighted arrow was found in the same house where Noah's diary was found, and it is in the author's collection of early tools.

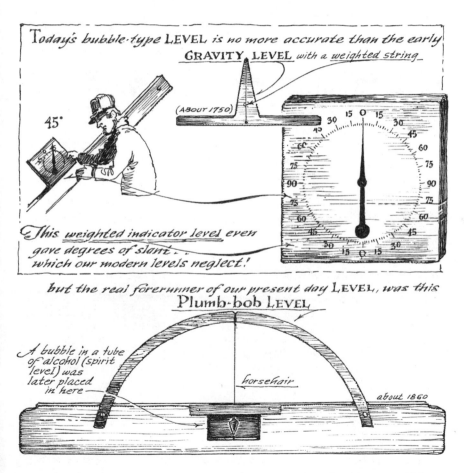

Today's bubble-type LEVEL is no more accurate than the early GRAVITY LEVEL with a weighted string

45°

(ABOUT 1750)

This weighted indicator level even gave degrees of slant... which our modern levels neglect!

but the real forerunner of our present day LEVEL, was this
Plumb-bob LEVEL

A bubble in a tube of alcohol (spirit level) was later placed in here —

horsehair

about 1860

28 : *A hot Sunday. Robert and I shall take our poles into the village next Tuesday. Mr. Adams says he will thatch our rick for us. First melons of the year at Sunday dinner.*

29 : *The rick is ready for Mr. Adams to thatch.*

30 : *Took waggon load of poles to the village with Robert Adams and collected four dollars from Mr. Minor.*

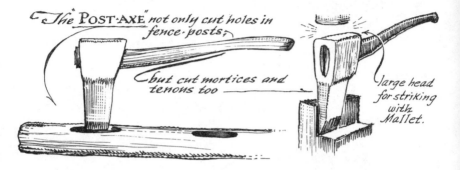

The POST·AXE not only cut holes in fence·posts,

but cut mortices and tenons too

large head for striking with Mallet.

Chapter 7

1 : Lammis Day, the first day of August. Our rick was not ready in time but the Adams family joined us and Mr. Adams spent the day in thatching. While sitting at the harvest table at noon, we saw the same two Indians looking on and we gave them as much food as they could carry away. Robert brought a maze game with him but only Sarah could do it.

Here the author thought "maze" was a misspelling of *maize* which is an old name for common corn. As Lammis Day involved the blessing of the first corn crop, it seemed possible that the "maze game" mentioned in the diary was some sort of corn game. But no; it was found that "maze games" were puzzles marked on paper or carved into wood, copying some famous labyrinth. For an example, we present "Rosamond's Bower" (or the "Maze at Woodstock"). It is an ingenious puzzle

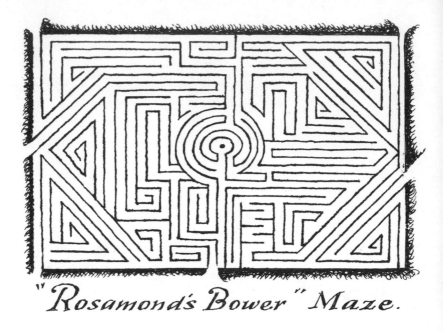

"Rosamond's Bower" Maze.

consisting of the problem of getting from one of the numerous outlets
to the bower in the center without crossing any of the lines. Turf mazes
were made during harvest festivals by turning up the sod into a maze
design to keep the youngsters busy at play while the parents ate and
drank at the tables. If making a turf maze was too difficult, or would
spoil a good hayfield, sheaves of wheat were laid out in a giant maze
at which even the adults might try their skill. The making of mazes became such a fad at one time in the late 16th century that the Puritans
banned all maze games by law, in an attempt to suppress "those folyshe
ceremonies."

> *2 : The two Indians returned this evening with gifts. They*
> *speak very little but they seem most friendly. They had*
> *dinner with us.*

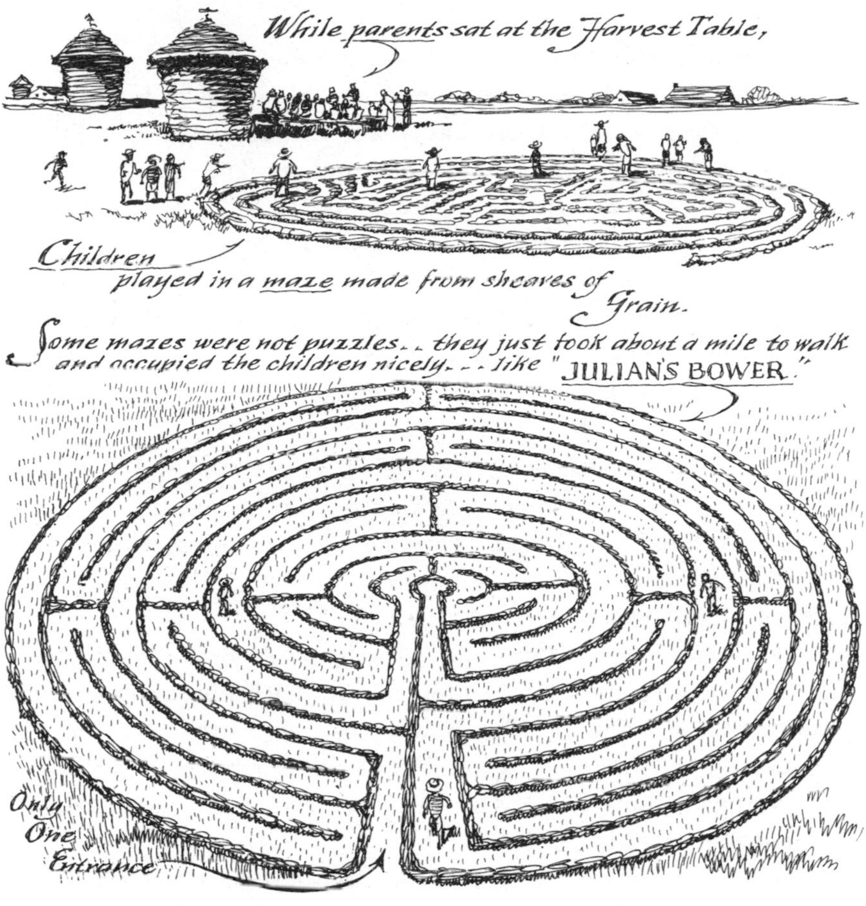

While parents sat at the Harvest Table,

Children played in a maze made from sheaves of Grain.

Some mazes were not puzzles... they just took about a mile to walk and occupied the children nicely. - - like "JULIAN'S BOWER."

Only One Entrance

Rachel saw them first, standing outside the window and peering inside.

"Quick Izaak," she whispered, "get your gun and close the shutters. There are Indians outside."

Izaak went to the window and recognized the Indians as those who had been to the harvest party yesterday.

79

"They are only calling," he said quietly. "And they seem to have gifts."

Without as much as a nod, and as soon as the door was opened, the two Indian men entered with a noiseless step, placed things on the table, and then stepped aside. There was an ash hunting bow, and a dish of sweet-fern, and a string of coarse wooden beads. The older man went again to the table and lifted the bow and pointed to Noah.

"Thank you," said Noah with a deep but nervous bow. The Indian could understand no English, it seemed. He neither smiled nor acknowledged Noah's bow, but he lifted the beads up and placed them over Rachel's head and then upon her neck.

"How wonderful!" she exclaimed with genuine pleasure. "What a nice thing to do!"

Next the Indian pointed at the sweet-fern and then at Izaak, who seemed bewildered, not knowing what to say or do with it.

"Thank them!" said Rachel. "They use sweet-fern to make a tea with. They say in the village that it cures the ague. They probably saw you sneezing and blowing your nose yesterday!"

After many smiles and gestures of satisfaction from the Blakes, none of which were returned by the silent Indians, Rachel brought out some fresh milk and cornbread. She drew benches up to the table and she signaled for the men to sit down. They took their pieces of bread and cups of milk, however, and walked quickly outside as if they were departing.

"Oh, they are taking my cups," said Rachel as quietly as she could. But as she followed them outside, she saw them sit on the ground near the doorway and begin to eat.

"Indians don't use chairs," said Izaak, "and if we want to be gracious hosts we must sit on the ground with them."

So Rachel and Izaak and Noah spent a good part of the afternoon doing what they never dreamed they would ever be doing: sitting on the bare ground, eating and drinking with guests.

Noah laughed openly at the scene and everyone seemed to have a good time, yet the Indians, who appeared never to have learned to laugh or even smile, did nothing but eat. Suddenly the two Indians stood up and left, without the slightest sort of departing gesture.

"I guess we shall never have worry about them," said Izaak, "so you can go back to leaving your shutters open during the summer nights. I certainly will never understand their ways, but they do have gratitude in their hearts; to me that makes them gentlemen."

"Amen to that," said Rachel. "I am so glad that we were civil to them yesterday. I must tell the Adamses about this."

3 : Very warm. The harvest fly was two days late.

On Lammis Day (the beginning of harvest time) the *cicada* was supposed to make its first appearance, or at least start its buzzing song. The cicada is what we now incorrectly call a locust, and what in Noah's time was called the Great Harvest Fly (mostly because it looks like an oversize version of the common housefly). Nowadays when people hear the "locust" singing in the trees during summertime, they will say it is "a sign of hot weather." This is actually a harkback to the ancient Lammis Day ceremony and its sayings.

Even today we find New England "harvest tables" on the market, not knowing just why they are called that. The first harvest tables were

Today's "HARVEST TABLE"

1800

was first a single plank Lammis Table

long narrow tables such as were reserved for Lammis Day gatherings. These gatherings resembled our present day Thanksgiving dinners in number and spirit. The tables were always made of one solid plank.

> *4 : The hottest of days. It is good for those who have not yet finished their harvest, but there was prayer for rain at Meeting today. The grass has become parched. We have moved even our bread into the cellar so drying is the summer warmth.*

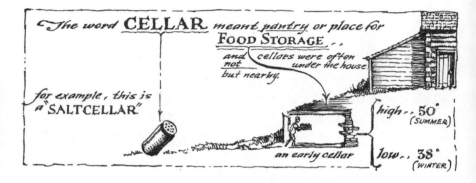

The cellar in Noah's time was not always under the house. It was more often off to one side. Usually it was on the north side of the house, and it was merely a room dug deep in the ground, with a dirt floor, for the storing of foods. *Cellar* was actually a mispronunciation of a French word *cella*, meaning *store-room*. The deepness of the underground store-room kept foods cool in summer yet warm enough to be above freezing in winter. The enclosed ice-box appeared and made the cella (or cellar) useless, and about that same time, the central furnace appeared. So the *cellar* has become the logical place for putting the heating system—a long way from what the word once implied!

> *5 : A fine thunderstorm arrived at noon. Garden work.*
> *6 : We have begun a corn cratch, and I have begun taking down the old forge barn.*

82

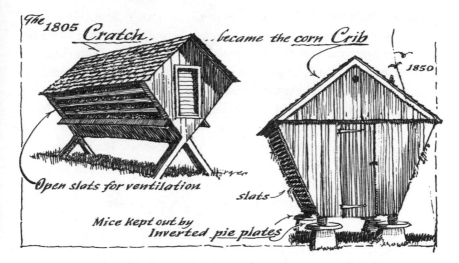

The 1805 *Cratch.* ..*became the corn* Crib

1850

Open slats for ventilation

slats

Mice kept out by Inverted pie plates

"The crop of corn will be so plentiful this year," said Izaak, "that we shall have no room for it in the loft. We shall make a good cratch to hold it."

"But can't we put the corn into the barn?" asked Noah.

"The purpose of a cratch," replied Izaak, "is to store the things in the open, yet keep it out of reach of mice or squirrels."

Cratch is an obsolete word, but what Izaak referred to was what we now call a *corn crib*. These open-slatted houses with outward slanting sides are for storing whole ears of corn and keeping them air-shrouded but dry. Since the mid 1800's these outbuildings have been built resting on large pie plates to keep mice from crawling up the foundation blocks, and the name corn *cratch* has changed to corn *crib*.

"We can use much of the forge barn material in building the cratch," Izaak told Noah, "and we must take care not to break the chimney bricks, for we shall have a stove in the mill this winter, and that will need a new chimney."

"A stove!" Noah thought out loud, "I've always hoped for a stove. The one the Adamses have in their place heats their kitchen so well during winter."

Stoves were scarce in back country villages, as almost every farmstead used fireplaces and brick ovens until the 1800's. Benjamin Franklin was perhaps the first to put a "fireplace into a box" which could be moved out into the room so that more heat might radiate from the same amount of fuel. In the 1790's the idea had been taken over so quickly and enthusiastically that many houses were built with a brick chimney starting up in the attic, and having numerous metal pipes leading from it to stoves in all the rooms.

The Adamses had been one of the first farm families to buy a stove, and Noah, as a boy of nine, had raced home to describe it.

"Oh, father!" he cried, "The Adamses have their fire locked up in a big black box, and it sits right in the middle of their room!"

The first American Heating Stove was fed from the Next room!

the PENNSYLVANIA "FIVE PLATE"

Bedroom

Kitchen fireplace

HOT ASHES

7 : The Forge barn is down. Only the chimney and forge remains. The bellows have been removed to the mill.

8 : Framed the corn cratch none too soon. Father has begun working in the corn fields.

9 : do.

10 : do.

11 : Sunday. Father's birthday. I presented him with a humorous toy. Mother baked a special pudding and Sarah joined us for dinner.

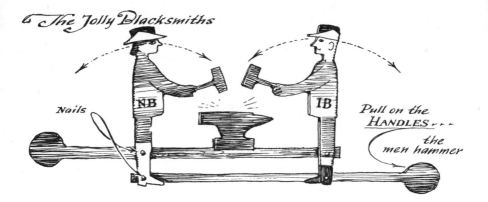

"Happy birthday father!" shouted Noah as he came to breakfast. "And here is a small gift for you that I have made by myself. When your mill is completed, it will remind you how we used to work at the anvil together. The one on the left is me and the handsome fellow on the right is you!"

"Thank you, son, and what a clever thing it is! I shall always keep it."

Izaak pulled the handles back and forth to see the two figures hammer on the anvil and he laughed aloud.

"It will always remind me that every time one of us works, so does the other—that we are a good team."

12 : A great degree of heat with thunder. But no rain.

13 : Worked in the corn fields.

14 : do.

15 : Mr. Beach arrived with a saw frame and a fine four foot blade. Its teeth are nearly two inches long.

16 : Father and Mr. Beach worked in the mill. I helped.

17 : do.

18 : Father and I went to Meeting without Mother who is ill.

85

Chapter 8

Here the diary is interrupted. A number of the center pages have been torn away and the next page begins on November sixth. Summer had passed and somewhere in the missing pages of the diary (on September 23rd to be exact), autumn had begun. The corn has now been cut and shocked, grain has been thrashed, all the hay is stacked, and the labors of summer are over. At this time of year all nature calls out from the wood-lots. Near the farm buildings the landscape becomes dotted with special apples like the Rambo, Maiden Blush, and Carolina Sweet. Off on the upper hillside, Rennets and Virginia Crabs and Cooper Russets show themselves on the thining orchard limbs. The insect chorus has reached its crescendo in the tall oatmeal-color grass that was green only yester-day.

The Blake mill now has been put together, and we find Izaak and Noah getting a shingle roof over it in time to protect the intricate wooden machinery from the late autumn rains.

*6 : Father and I have the mill roof all but shingled. It is fun
working at night, but the weather is most cold.*

"This moon is brighter than the harvest moon," said Isaak, "and that
is because of the crisper, colder air. It is even brighter than last month's
Hunter's Moon, I think."

"Why do they call it the Hunter's Moon?" asked Noah.

"I suppose because it occurs at the right time to light the forest during the good hunting season. Though gentle people like us, who seldom use the gun, usually refer to it as the Worker's Moon. That is because it is the best time to do outdoor farm work at night before the cold sets in."

"Well," said Noah, "the cold has certainly set in with this full moon. Isn't this our second heavy frost of the year?"

"That it is," replied Izaak as he pushed another packet of shingles toward his son and stopped to rub his hands together in the cold night air. "They say that Sham Summer (Indian Summer) begins right after the first frost, and that was during the last full moon. It looks like winter is nearing and 'most upon us."

Just then there was a call from the direction of the house, from Rachel.

"Time for a warm drink, men! Come down from that roof before you catch your deaths. It is near midnight!"

Over a cup of steaming sassafras tea and a plate of cornbread, Noah and Izaak felt the satisfaction of having done a good day's work.

"I can't see why you must work on a slanting roof at night," said Rachel. "Just because the almanac says it's the best time for shingling. It sounds silly and dangerous to me!"

"Oh come now!" said Izaak. "We are not as superstitious as all that. We just work best in the cold of the evening. And shingles left to dry out their first time in the heat of midday, are apt to curl. There are a lot of moonlore sayings full of common sense, and there are a lot full of hearsay and nonsense too."

"Well I think we should sort them out and not bring up a son on anything but knowledge and good sense."

Noah laughed, but he had no retort. He was comfortably tired, and the hearth was warming him to sleep. It had been a good day, and a good night.

When he went to his room and blew out the candle, the moon lit the room so well that he looked about for a second or so, seeking another candle to blow out. And when he drew the covers up to make a tent to build up body warmth, the moon danced a silly dance through the bubbles of his window pane.

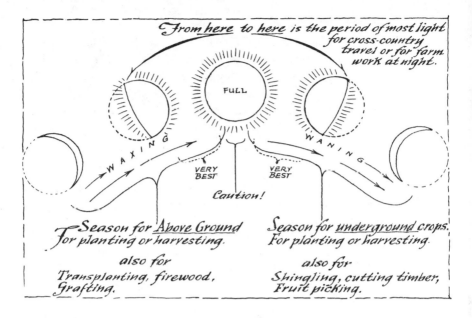

What a pleasure it is, he thought, to spice the world with things like moonlore and weatherlore. The moon is an exact timepiece that will never change, and the seasons will always be with us; yet not to be sure about tomorrow's weather is more of a joy than a worry; and to wonder about the moon is an unending pleasure of life. If ever man should find his way there and learn everything about the moon, would the loss be greater than the accomplishment? It was a profound thought to go to sleep on.

> 7 : *Finished the mill roof in time for a rain.*
> 8 : *Windy and chilly weather. Closing in the open places with strips.*
> 9 : *Spent the day closing in the mill.*
> 10 : *Sunday. Robert Adams will come over tomorrow to help us with the apples.*
> 11 : *Spent the day gathering apples. Robert stayed over.*

89

12 : More work in the orchard.

*13 : Gathered cyder apples. Will drive them to the village to-
morrow and deliver Robert to his home. Shall dinner with
the Adams and Sarah.*

The Blake orchards were a scattering of trees rather than a set plot, for Izaak wanted first to grow trees of special fruits before he transplanted seedlings into a patterned orchard. The "cyder" apples were of a dwarf type known as *crab;* a crab apple in Noah's time was not like the crab apple of today, as the word crab merely meant it was a wild variety. The eating apples were known as Russet, Golden, Ribston, and Normandy. All the eating apples of 1805 were "pippins" because they were raised from a pip (apple seed), although now we think of a "pippin" as just one kind of apple.

It seems a pity nowadays that the American apple tree has lost much favor as a useful landscape tree. For a full century the early American worked at cultivating apple trees, and you can still see the evidences wherever the landscape has not been "developed" and "improved." Walking through any wooded area, you will come upon a few ancient apple trees, and they will always mark the place where a farmhouse once stood. If children in this country made the effort of starting orchards, even one tree to each child, what an interesting project it would be, and what a contribution it would be to the nation!

". Where a farmhouse once stood "

Robert Adams and Noah Blake first picked the eating apples. These were picked very carefully from the stem, using cotton gloves or without using the hands. The least pulling or squeezing, according to the

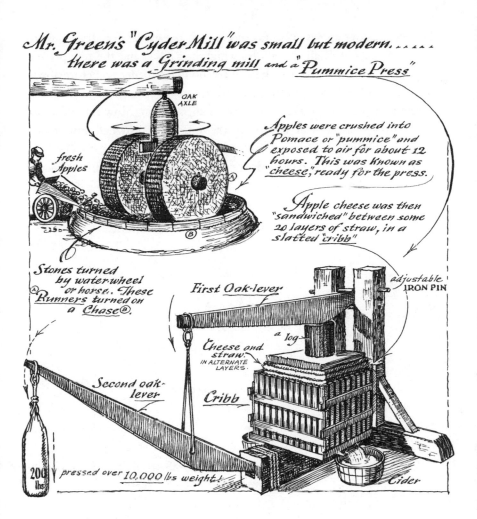

Mr. Green's "Cyder Mill" was small but modern ......
there was a *Grinding mill* and a "*Pummice Press*"

OAK AXLE

fresh Apples

Apples were crushed into Pomace or "pummice" and exposed to air for about 12 hours. This was known as "*cheese*", ready for the press.

Apple cheese was then "sandwiched" between some 20 layers of straw, in a slatted "*cribb*"

Stones turned by water-wheel or horse.. These *Runners* turned on a *Chase* ⓐ.

First Oak-lever

adjustable IRON PIN

Cheese and straw: IN ALTERNATE LAYERS.

a log

Second oak-lever

Cribb

200 lbs

pressed over 10,000 lbs weight

Cider

old ways, rendered the apple unfit for whole winter storage. These apples were put stem up in a straw-packed box and taken into the cellar as soon as frost threatened them. There they were put on stone (very often native marble) shelves (wood shelves were never used). One apple was never allowed to touch another while in storage. When all the prime eating apples were taken care of, the apples for drying were picked. Then, last of all, the apples which had fallen and the few poorer apples still left on the tree. These were doomed to decay before long, so they were used for applesauce and for vinegar.

One may see why there was a law against cutting down apple trees in the earliest American days, for the one tree provided raw fruit, cider for drinking, apple sauce, dried fruit, and vinegar.

Early apple trees were trained to grow low, so pickers did not always use ladders. But in New England there was once a chair-ladder that

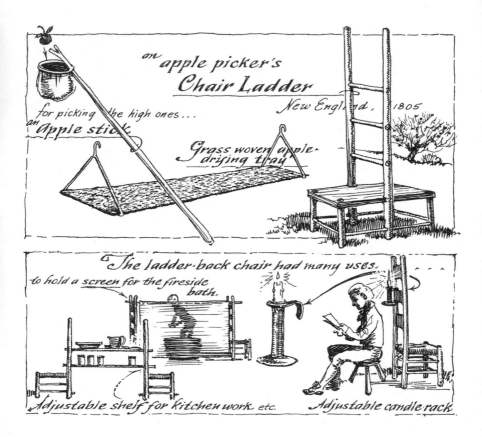

an apple picker's Chair Ladder
New England, 1805

for picking the high ones...
an apple stick

Grass woven apple-drying tray

The ladder-back chair had many uses.

to hold a screen for the fireside bath.

Adjustable shelf for kitchen work. etc.

Adjustable candle rack

could either be stood upon or climbed, and was light enough to carry about. These were rough farm devices, so there are very few left to be found; they were nothing like the well-made ladder-chair, which was a piece of indoor furniture. It has been said, however, that the ladder-chair might have been designed from the chair-ladder device. (The author, who collected ladder-chairs, was intrigued with the frequent burns he found on the backs of such chairs; not until he visited a back-woods home in New Hampshire and saw someone using a ladder-chair as an adjustable candle rack, did he solve the mystery. This also explains the reason for the projecting lip on many old candlesticks which hitherto was thought to be simply a handle for carrying it.)

> *14 : Bang drove a great load of apples to Mr. Green's cyder mill. Bang is lighter than Daniel and I fear we shall need a drag-shoe for the waggon. Had dinner at the Adams. Sarah had a letter from her home in Pennsylvania. Her parents wish her to return.*

The drag-shoe or ruggle is an obsolete piece of wagon hardware that few people know about today. It was hung in front of the rear wheels, and when, in going downhill, a heavy load threatened to roll forward and push the horse over, the iron shoe was slid under the wheel (one wheel or both rear wheels). Then the back part of the wagon became a sled, and the horse actually pulled the load downhill. This, of course, was before the addition of wheel-brakes to wagons.

The Drag Shoe — *was released on going down a steep hill with a very heavy load.* TO HAND LEVER. *and the wheel ran right up onto the shoe.*

15 : Stayed over at the Adams house, to work the same amount of time that Robert worked helping me.

16 : Finished at the Adams and returned home.

18 : Sunday. Mother had begun apple-drying yesterday. I hope Sarah does not go home.

It is interesting to note that Robert first helped the Blakes, and then Noah helped the Adamses. This was a custom practiced religiously in the early farm days; when there was a job that took more than one person, a group of people did the work, not for pay, but to get that same kind of job done for themselves later. In that way, there was no hiring of help. For example, when a harvest mowing job was ready, some eight men showed up at the designated farm and did the whole job in one day. Then each of the eight men was entitled to the same service on his own farm. Food and switchel (drinks) were the obligation of the farmer whose land was being worked. For a farmer to hire help to raise a barn or frame a house was unheard of. Cooperative labor was the answer.

Apple drying is a practice long forgotten. Yet you may take almost any fruit nowadays and dry it into slices that can be eaten raw or sugared. It is still a good way to make apples keep into the winter. You may often see hooks in the ceiling beams near the fireplaces of old houses; they were used for hanging a long tray of apple slices where the heat of the fire could effectively dry them out and seldom were the drying trays empty. These same hooks were the ones which held a tent of blankets around the fire to house the Saturday-night bather.

19 : A day of high winds. Father believes that many nuts have fallen from the woodlot trees and he suggests that we gather them before the squirrels do.

20 : Went to the woodlot with Bang, and wheeled in several logs we had left to season for flooring. Father will try out the new sawmill with them.

21 : Our first log was cut today. Father says he will save the center piece for a harvest table. The noise was so loud that Mr. Adams heard it and came over to see. Mother and Father are pleased with the saw, but Father says the wheel ratio must be changed. I asked Mr. Adams to send Robert over tomorrow for nutting.

22 : *Robert and I spent the day nutting. We gathered four baskets of chestnuts and about half as many walnuts.*

23 : *Gathered almost twice the amount today as yesterday. Our hands are dyed dark brown from the nut juice.*

24 : *Sunday. Went to Meeting. Sarah was amused with my stained hands which will not clean. I told her that I hope she does not return home.*

25 : *Father cut several boards for the new floor but I had a great disappointment for I thought we would have the wood floor this year. Father says the boards must season for nearly one year! Mother is disappointed too, but she is accustomed to the dirt floor and wants it for one more Christmas.*

26 : *Mr. Green came out with four barrels of cyder that he has pressed from our apples. The barrels are from Mr. Minor and I think I recognize some of the hoop-pole material that Robert and I sold to him.*

27 : *Father is making a smaller pinion wheel for the saw machinery.*

Boring through white oak must have taken a great deal of strength, yet there never seemed to be much complaint from the old-time builders. When you think that the pointed screw was not thought of until the mid 1800's, it seems remarkable that metal bits could be made to bore through the toughness of seasoned oak. The drawing shows a smith's beam drill such as Izaak Blake must have used in his shop. With such a contrivance, you could put more weight on the drill than the complete weight of your body. Below you may see some of the bits used a century or more ago with the beam drill. Bits of this type can now be bought for use with electric drill sets; they are called "new high speed bits," but Noah Blake knew them well.

Although wooden gear wheels, like those in the machinery of old water mills, were not perfectly made, they became perfect through actual wear.

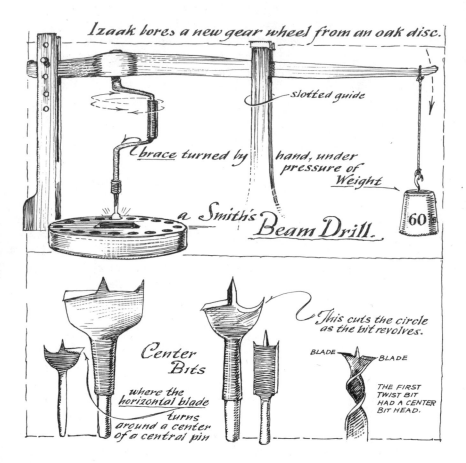

Izaak bores a new gear wheel from an oak disc.

slotted guide

brace turned by hand, under pressure of Weight

a Smith's **Beam Drill.**

60

This cuts the circle as the bit revolves.

Center Bits

where the horizontal blade turns around a center of a central pin

BLADE — BLADE

THE FIRST TWIST BIT HAD A CENTER BIT HEAD.

Before very long, a set of noisy gears would wear themselves into smoothness and quietness, which is something metal gears will not do.

> *28 : Snow! The first white of the year. We are looking to the sleds which are in sad repair.*
> *30 : Spent the day in the mill helping Father.*

Chapter 9

1 : December has arrived with another fall of snow—just enough to cover the ground. Went to Meeting in the wagon but we soon look forward to introducing Bang to runners. Father says it shall be my job to keep the bridge floor in snow. The bridge bears my name, he reminded me.

Very few people stop to think how important it was to keep snow shoveled into the old covered bridges. In fact, some believe they were built just to keep out the snow. Yet because most road traffic was during the winter (because of the impassability of muddy summer or spring roads, and the ease with which heavy loads could be sledded over snow), the covered bridge's busiest time was sled time. A load of logs stuck in a bridge for lack of snow on the floor could tie up the traffic badly.

"We shall miss Daniel this winter," said Noah. "He pulled the snow roller as if he were two oxen. I don't think Bang could even budge it!"

"Well, this year we'll have to leave the snow rolling up to the village.

We've given them a good new bridge; I guess they won't mind helping with the roadway now."

2 : Banked the house with cornstalks and pompion vines.

It seems a little late to bank the house, yet Noah has had a busy time of it, and better late than never. A thick matting of cornstalks around the bottom of the house will keep some of the winter cold and wind out. "Pompion" was the old name referring to the pumpkin which was used mostly for cattle fodder. It is a little confusing to learn that the old picture of the pioneer American with his pumpkin pie and his Thanksgiving dinner, is quite incorrect. You will notice that Noah's diary went completely through November without a mention of Thanksgiving. Only when Lincoln set aside a Thanksgiving day in 1863, did the almanacs begin to list the holiday. Thanksgiving began as a Puritan day, but because the Puritans were opposed to Christmas as a holiday, the American farmer looked down upon anything Puritan, and he was content with his harvest thanksgiving feasts in August.

3 : I had a long talk with Mother about Sarah. Mother is go-
ing to ask Sarah to stay for Christmas. The weather is
warmer and the snow has disappeared.
4 : I have started making rockers for a chair to give Sarah for
Christmas.

"Do you think she will like to have her own chair?" asked Noah.

Rachel herself had always wanted a rocker, so she was being honest. "I cannot imagine a nicer present!"

Rockers were not exactly new in 1805, but nearly all of them were converted chairs. Most of the rockers at that time were slat-back chairs with oversize rockers exactly like those beneath a child's cradle. It is quite possible that in 1805 the rocking chair was only twenty-five years old. It's origin is not certain, but it is American—possibly the only completely American piece of furniture.

The Rocking Chair . . an American invention

. . most rocking chairs were plain chairs with rockers added in the late 1700's.

Pilgrim type.

1690-1700

Comb-back Windsor

1790-1805

Slat-back ladder Rocker for Sarah Trowbridge.

1805

Pennsylvania 1790

Giant Dutch Rocker

1800

Cradle type Rocker

1780

Noah had taken his share of the hoop-pole money and while in the village he had bought the kind of a chair he thought Sarah would like; the rockers were an afterthought.

5 : The saw mill machinery is complete. Father and I have begun to close in the walls and start a brick chimney in preparation for a stove. The forge fire will pipe into the same chimney.

6 : *Same work. It is almost too cold for the plaster.*
7 : *Chimney-building still!*
8 : *Mother spoke with Sarah at Meeting today. I do not know what she said and she will not say. The Meeting was cold. I wish they would place a stove there. They need that more than a bell.*

Noah did not know who was buying it, but it was announced that a bell had been ordered for the village Meeting House, and some day soon it would arrive, having come all the way from Boston. It was Izaak's secret idea when he first began building his house; he was away from the village and that was good—but he wanted to be near enough to hear an alarm. In those days the town bells told of fires and deaths and funerals and holidays and feasts and church events and Indian attacks. Bells were not just for the pleasure. Yet to hear a fine bell peal across the rich countryside is the greatest music to the farmer, and Izaak was a farmer. He had seen an advertisement in the *Massachusetts Spy* or *Worcester Gazette*. "Church bells," it had read, "of all sizes." So he had

"*He had seen an advertisement*"

HERE are a few old time Church Bell Codes

Church bells rang at 7 A.M., at 12 noon and 9 P.M. (CURFEW)

Deaths were tolled: 6 bells for a woman, 9 for a man. After a pause, the deceased's age was tolled in bells.

Births tolled after 7 A.M. tolling.

After 9 p.m. (curfew toll) the day of the month in bells was rung (10 bells for the 10th etc.)

CHURCH BELLS.

PAUL REVERE & SON,
No. 13, Lynn Street, North End, BOSTON,

HAVE conſtantly for ſale, CHURCH and ACADEMY BELLS, of all ſizes, which they will warrant *equal* to any made in Europe, or this *country.* From perſonal information obtained in Europe, and twenty years experience, they are aſſured they can give ſatis-faćtion, and will ſell, on as good terms, as they can be imported for, or obtained in this country.

sent in an order for a smallish bell, and it was to be inscribed: "To the village from Rachel and Izaak Blake and from their son Noah." Even now it was being so inscribed at Number 13 Lynn Street, North End, Boston, by a very expert bell maker named Paul Revere. And if it arrived before December 25th, it would be a Christmas surprise.

> *9 : Wonderful news! Robert Adams came over with a note from Sarah. She has received word from her home that she may stay over the Christmas days, and that her Mother and Father are already on their way here. I went to see Sarah after my work and I expressed my joy.*

"Why didn't you tell me you'd asked to stay?" asked Noah.

"I wanted to wait till the reply came," said Sarah. "And besides, I wanted to surprise you. If I'd gone back home, I would have had to stay the whole year, and I should not care for that at all."

> *10 : Began building a sled for Bang to pull. Father is using four of the wide oak boards that he intended for the new house flooring, to make the sled floor.*

"Won't it need seasoning?" asked Noah. "I thought you said it would take about a year to season those boards."

"No" said Izaak, "not if they are to stay out in the weather continually. Only boards for placing indoors need seasoning. These boards will season nicely right on the sled. But do help me with the metal runners. They are almost ready for me to put onto the sled skids."

They went into the "under-room" of the mill, where for two days Izaak had been feeding a small fire in the forge basin just to warm the new chimney and help the plaster to harden and keep it from freezing. It wasn't a fire big enough to warm the place, but there were still glowing embers. Reaching out of a window after swinging open its wooden shutter, Izaak pulled a rope and fastened the end to a peg. This opened the gate in the sluice. At once there was a splashing of water somewhere

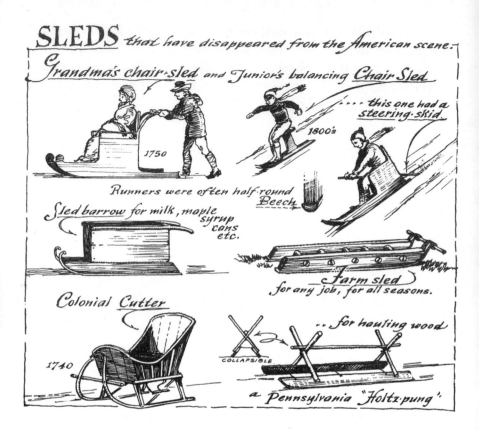

SLEDS *that have disappeared from the American scene.*

Grandma's chair-sled and Junior's balancing **Chair Sled**

· · · this one had a steering-skid

1800's

Runners were often half-round Beech

1750

Sled barrow for milk, maple syrup cans etc.

Farm sled for any job, for all seasons.

Colonial Cutter

1740

COLLAPSIBLE

·· for hauling wood

a Pennsylvania "Holtz-pung".

outside, and before another minute, there came the groan and squeak of wood turning against wood. The mill wheel was "under way." The wood was not old enough to have worn itself into the smoothness of a nearly perfect wheel, so there were unnatural rumblings and shudderings now and then that caused Izaak to cock his head and listen. It was like listening to the breathing of a first-born child. Then he stopped listening, and his face assumed a pleased expression.

"Before long she will turn as slick and easy as, any wheel!" he said.

He swung a wooden lever over against an oaken cog that protruded from the big main axle beam, and twice during each revolution, just as

102

Izaak had planned, that cog lifted the bellows and then released it. The strong breathing of the bellows wakened the embers in the forge basin, and before the mill wheel had revolved a dozen times, the coals were alive and hissing.

11 : *Our first business at the mill! An order for sawing some pine floor boards, for Mr. Thoms.*
12 : *Worked at the saw mill. Pine wood cuts beautifully.*
13 : *do.*
14 : *We took off the day. General Washington died this day six years ago. We could hear a cannon salute all the way from the village, and Robert told me there was a service held there.*
15 : *At Sunday Meeting I came across a Biblical verse which I copied and gave to Sarah. I asked her not to open it until she arrived at her room. Now I am very worried about it.*

All the way home from Meeting, Noah had thought of nothing but what he had done. His father noticed a faraway look on Noah's face.

"Keep the wagon out of those ruts, son," he said. "You must be thinking of something a long way off!"

Noah set his mind back to driving Bang as a horse should be driven from Meeting of a Sunday. Still he did keep trying to remember the quotation that he had copied from The Second Epistle of John. It went:

"And now I beseech thee, lady, not as though I wrote a new commandment unto thee, but that which we had from the beginning, that we love one another."

16 : *No word from Sarah. A soft snow fell today and I worked at making firewood before the snow becomes too heavy.*
17 : *The snow stopped and I still am at splitting wood. No word from Sarah yet.*
18 : *Mr. Thoms' order has been done. It has been loaded upon a sled and is waiting for a snow.*

"I think we should make a small offering at Sunday service," said

Izaak, "out of what Mr. Thoms pays us. It was our first sawmill job and I am exceedingly proud of the water wheel and its machinery. That saw went through pine much easier than it did with the oak for our flooring. Yet I would not have pine for a floor, because it should not be nailed down until a year or more after it is laid. My father had a pine floor, and I shall always remember that year of toe-stubbing that I endured.

Indeed, it was the old custom to lay floor boards down loosely and to nail them only after they had dried completely in the warmth of a winter household. Often when the boards dried and shrank, the whole series of floor boards would need sliding over until they were all tight. Then a new narrow board would have to be added to complete the floor before the final nailing took place. "Random widths" do mark an ancient floor, but random shapes mark them even more distinctly, for the early boards were seldom the same width at one end as they were at the other.

The early random-floors were random more in *Shapes,* than regular width.

wide		narrow
18"		20"
16"		18"
20"		16"

Square nails are still best (and are used) for floors (THEY WON'T SPLIT)
The old PLANCHER *Nails* had clinching heads — for floors.

19 : Mother has begun Christmas baking and the smell is wonderful. It snowed, though not enough to sled Mr. Thoms' boards. No word yet from Sarah.

20 : A great surprise today! The bell that Father ordered arrived in the village. It was drawn by a waggon with four horses, and it took eight men to lift it down.

"It is a beauty!" said Izaak when he arrived with Noah to help. "We must not tell Mother until she hears it ring. When do you think we can get it into a belfry?" he asked.

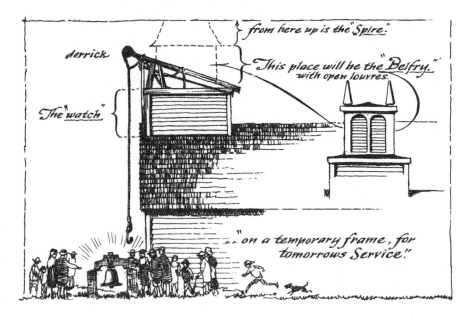

Mr. Simon, the town framer and carpenter, said a derrick would be needed. "We will hoist it up on the watch-tower platform," he said, "and then we shall build a belfry wall around it. Some folks will want to see a spire on top of the belfry, but we can't do that for a while."

"We'll get it up on a temporary frame," said another man, "and we shall ring it for services tomorrow."

21 : What a day! They started ringing the bell as we drove to the village. Mother was most surprised and everyone con-

gratulated Father. I saw Sarah and when the Service was finished she gave me a folded paper asking me to open it when I got home, which I did. It just said first chapter of Ruth, 16.

Noah had known that the piece of paper held good news, for Sarah smiled through what seemed to be a blush when she gave it to him. And all during the service, whenever he looked at Sarah, she had that same strange expression upon her face.

Noah didn't wait until evening to read his note. As soon as they were home, after he had unhitched Bang and had the harness hung, he went to that corner of the barn where an open window cast a ray of light into the hay-filled room. Then he opened the note and read its message. It mystified him and he went to the house, still wondering.

"Mother," he asked, "where is our Bible?"

"It is where it should be, in the Bible box," said Rachel. "Are you going to read it?"

"Well," said Noah, "I just wanted to look up something. I want to see the sixteenth verse of the first chapter of Ruth."

"You don't have to look that up," said Rachel, "I know it by heart!"

"You do?" asked Noah, looking very surprised, "How does it go?"

"It is what Ruth said, and it goes: 'Entreat me not to leave thee, or to return from following after thee: for whither thou goest, I will go: and where thou lodgest, I will lodge: thy people will be my people, and thy God my God.'"

"Is *that* what it says? Are you sure?" Noah didn't wait for a reply. He had already left the room.

"Where are you going?" called Rachel. "Dinner is almost ready!"

"I'm going over to the Adamses," shouted Noah, who was already out of the house and heading down the path.

"What in the world is wrong with Noah?" asked Izaak, who had just turned into the doorway. "He seems in a great hurry to leave."

"Nothing is wrong. I guess everything is right. I guess Sarah told him. Are you ready for a bit of dinner, future father-in-law?"

106

the winter of 1805

CORN FIELD
THE BARN
IZAAK
LOG CART
Banking
RACHEL
CELLAR
SARAH
SLED
NOAH
the new mill
THE ROOF ON THE BRIDGE
The old water wheels froze tight during winter.

Snow rolling to make a smooth highway for sleds.

22 : Shortest day of the year, Midwinter Day. Finished Sarah's rocking chair. Made Mother a candlestick.

Noah had gone to the under-room of the mill to start up the fire, only to find his father already working at the forge. Both had the same idea— to make a Christmas candlestick for Rachel.

107

"You have already started one!" said Noah in disappointment.

"I didn't know that you were going to give Mother the same thing," said Izaak, "but why don't you make a matching stick? Then she could have a fine pair of candlesticks for Christmas. I'm sure she'd like nothing better."

> 23 : *Draped the room with laurel leaves on a string. Everything is set for Christmas. Sarah's parents should arrive tomorrow.*
>
> 24 : *It was a fine Day Before Christmas. Sarah's parents arrived and I met them. They are good people and I hope they approve of me.*

Noah left off with that thought. He snuffed out the candle and suddenly the smell of bayberry filled the room. He knew then that his mother had put this special candle in his room for the holiday occasion. Everything seemed perfect now. He could hear the crackling of the fire in the next room and his father returning from the barn after putting Bessie and Bang "to bed." He remembered how on this night all animals were supposed to speak. On Christmas Eve the livestock are supposed to discuss their master, after the manner in which they were said to have done of the Great Master in the manger at Bethlehem. He wondered what Bessie and Bang might say.

He looked out of his window, but there was no moon. A few crystals of snow blew against the glass from the dark outer world. The winter of 1805 had taken over the American landscape.

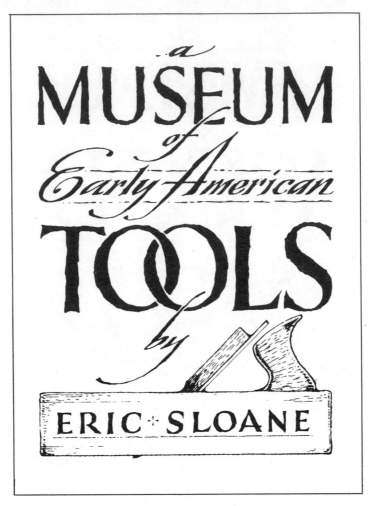

a MUSEUM
of
Early American
TOOLS
by
ERIC · SLOANE

This uniquely illustrated study of craftsmen
in Colonial America discusses early tools and artifacts
used by wheelwrights, coopers, blacksmiths,
and many other proud and individualistic craftsmen
of the pre-industrial age. (5¼″ x 8″)
$2.95 / 24675